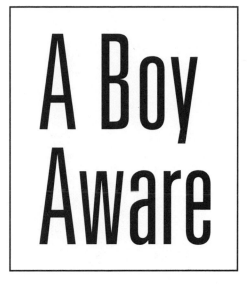

A Boy Aware

ON BEING FIFTEEN

THE SELECTED POEMS

Geoffrey Dilenschneider

New Millennium Press

First published in the United States of America in 2002
by New Millennium Entertainment, Inc.
301 N. Canon Drive #214
Beverly Hills, CA 90210

Library of Congress Cataloging-in-Publication Data available upon request.
ISBN: 1-893224-51-1

Jacket design by Kerry DeAngelis, KL Design
Interior design by Carolyn Wendt

Printed in the United States of America

10 9 8 7 6 5 4 3 2

꒰

Dedicated always to my girl, Katheryn French
and to my brother, Peter, for always annoying the hell out of me

꒰

IN REMEMBRANCE

On either side of me stands one tower,
So high and proud
In every window stand a thousand people,
So free and loud,
Yelling silent thoughts of sadness to my soul,
Lost of a common goal,
Broken of the things that God once said to be,
Forgotten in a sea of timelessness and animosity . . .

But nowhere will we be going
Without a sadness showing:
Penetrating through the fabrics
Of our lives
And of our days
And of our wives
And of our ways,
The thoughts will go on being
Of the lost of hearts a-beating . . .
        In memory

ACKNOWLEDGMENTS

I would like to lovingly acknowledge and thank my Creative Writing class for listening to all that I read and sung in class. To Mrs. Sorensen, for your encouragement unheeded by the modern day.

I really want to thank Mara and Mike, Amanda, Dan, Leo, Steve, Adam, Kelsey, Alice, and John . . . Erin, Kim, Andrew, Lexi, Francesca, Angela, Rob, Marika, and Amanda C, for being my sort of test-dummies, helping me realize that courage and discipline have always been there inside me; it was just a matter of realizing it.

Thanks to Mara Hertz, just for saying hello and for showing me that no matter who a person is, you should always be kind to them.

I want to thank Katie Bennett, for inspiring me a thousand and seven trillion times, putting me at levels of thought until then unknown to me, and not even meaning to. For blushing every time I told you that. You unwittingly helped develop my skill, retain knowledge about my writing, enhance my technique, and keep my eyes open for new ideas. You helped keep the days happy free of quiet hate and anger and helped create a sense of tranquil limbo where neither the physical self nor the spiritual self nor the mental self had more control than the others. You helped alleviate the pains and bores of scholastics while heightening the awareness of self and every positive aspect of life. Dedicated to you, Katie, for laughing at my jokes, for smiling at my smile, for listening to my words, and for not listening when I interrupted your conversations with someone else. For your bright outlook, and for your attitude of "the glass is totally full." And for the spirit of your pure heart, who's virtue will let your life lead as you please, and for how it's humble greatness translates into my life's story, making it that much richer. You are my greatest inspiration.

Thanks to my mother, for her protagonist support, her love, and her encouragement; also for her great orange juice during those hard mornings.

The greatest thanks to my father, for all the precious time he spends helping me in every way he can, and for his words of truth, wisdom, reality, and on how and why to slow down.

Lastly, to Katheryn, for whom words cannot even begin to describe. In everyone, every day, I see you always; the gentle reminder of the person I met on an eight-day cruise in the Baltic Sea, who I realized was the sweetest, kindest, most honest and loving soul on the face of this earth. You are the most precious gem in the world to me: there, but not; forever in mind, but so far away.

CONTENTS

❋

CHAPTER 6: The Buildup and the Breakdown

CHAPTER I

THE BEGINNING

I THINK

※

You are not connected . . . to anything.
You are not connected to anything because you are connected to everything.
How can I be connected to anything, how can I put my own mind to rest,
When my mind is not just my own, but is public property?
The property of every atom and molecule and compound that exists!
I want to satisfy myself, but I don't just exist as myself,
I'm just a storage room for certain things that the Guy upstairs needed to
store for his hibernation period when he couldn't manage everything,
So he just stuck things into one of his saving accounts.
And he saw that the saving account was good. . . !
He then met us halfway and gave us this stupid thing called sentience and/or
free will.
The will for a machine that only exists for a specific purpose to operate as a
different, more essential, less out-dated machine, yet he still cannot imagine
himself as anything other than a machine.
Machines always date,
And more complex, durable, efficient machines always take their places.
Whatever has a purpose, it is a machine.
I wish reason and rhyme would not exist,
I think that in your heart of hearts, you do too.
But as machines, created in the image of the inventor,
There's no way that we could imagine things without rhyme or reason,
Because even imagination is the slave to those.
There is no rhyme or reason to rhyme or reason.
They are there, and they are inescapable.
And here we are trying to create order out of chaos,
But there is no order in chaos,
Because neither exists, but are merely an illusion.
Chaos is the illusion of the mind,
And order that exists is the only thing that exists as well.
The only number that exists is one.
There is no other purpose.
Damn order!

Damn chaos!
Just forget about the whole thing and let's move on with the illusion!
But I don't want any more illusions, I want the truth!
But when you are just a transitory parable for the eternal, what the hell else are
you going to get?
That's unreasonable to expect,
There is nothing to be ashamed of,
And nothing to be proud of either,
Chained to death,
Yet chained to life,
Chained to every opposite that is!
There is nothing to prevent me,
But nothing to encourage me,
Everything is a jumbled mess,
And there is nothing but that jumbled mess in any mess.
Even the 'cleanest' room has things growing in it that nobody sees.
Why even talk about this!
It's so fucking dumb!
There is nothing that will get me anywhere,
But the 'dialogue' keeps going until I can no longer sustain to have it.
There is so little to be found or said,
So little to be done,
But so much that needs to be done,
And there is no way to get past it,
Because every time you get past it,
You get to something else.
SLAVE! SLAVE! SLAVE!
And then you have to keep going,
Searching for the light at the end of the never ending tunnel,
And when you think you've found the light,
You've only found its reflection.
And then you keep on going down the tunnel,
But the light is never found,
And it's true that the light's reflection produces more light,
But there is only so much light one can take before you go blind!
And after that, burn yourself, maybe to death.

So you just settle for a certain amount of light before and after the end of
the consequences.
And the consequences are always there and following us.
And never drawing back from the territory they claim for themselves.
And they just keep going and going and going.
And the band keeps on playing and playing and playing.

There is always weather,
There are always colors,
There are always numbers,
There are always shapes,
A circle is always 360 degrees.
And at once I am thankful and resentful of those facts.
And I cannot ever go to the ends of the earth,
Because eventually I will be right back where I started,
And I cannot go to the ends of space because there's always a place not only a
little bit further, but much, much further.
And there is always a place within reach,
But there is always infinite numbers of others that are never in reach.
I go to sleep,
And almost always wake up (and I guess I should be thankful for that)
But when I wake up, I'm only a little more awake than when I went to sleep,
And when I wake up from that,
I guess I'm no longer me,
If I were more awake, I would sleep even less,
I don't know whether that's good or bad. I really don't.
And then there is nothing to be done because the ends of the earth are not
really ends,
And there is always too far and further to go,
And there is never a stop
Throughout everything I just have to move on and on and on.
Never stopping until the cows come home to mama and papa and the family.
The safety net of security is not secure,
And can never be because there is always something bigger,
Just when you think you're on top,
There's somebody with something more powerful.

I guess I could kill the mortal part,
And I wonder what would happen to the immortal,
Is it really immortal? I wonder.
I don't know because there is too little to really tell the difference among men
and women,
But there is nothing to be done about everything,
And nothing to be done about nothing,
And vice-versa.
And the interference picks up and one can't concentrate on one's immortal
Part and must sustain the mortal if the immortal is to attain satisfaction,
And while one can minimize it, one cannot do anything truly to eradicate it,
Because eradication would eradicate everything.
So what would I do to purge myself of sins that would not have been
Committed in another situation,
And the state to war continues . . .
Everybody says to end war, but nobody does,
I don't think we can. If we could, we'd stop.
War is needed to live, and we correct ourselves,
And give anything to ourselves that would restore the order that unfortunately
we need to survive,
But the cosmos are but parable as well,
Everything is a concept impossible to know about when one is remotely finite,
There is something out there . . .
Something past God,
Past the universe,
Even past the imagination.
I'm incapable of figuring out what it is,
I'm also incapable of ceasing to try to figure out what it is,
That is who I am,
And who you are,
And what everything is,
But nothing.*

ᴥ

"The hardest thing in the whole big wide world is to keep secrets or pain
bottled up inside yourself. The easiest thing in the world is to let them all out
by talking to someone about them. Being that someone is a burden of sorts,
but brings both of those people closer together."

ᴥ

DEFINE 'NORMAL'

✻

do you ever get the feeling
that nobody understands what you do?
I do.
do you ever get the feeling
that nobody understands why you do it?
I do.
do you ever get the feeling
that nobody understands you, period?
I do.
have you ever confronted your father
and told him straight out
what you have felt about him
for the last six years?
I just did.
have you ever had your father
distrust and not believe you?
I have.
have you ever had your father
say goodbye to you
in that one way
that just breaks your heart?
I did.

have you ever screamed at your father
that you love him
because you hate him
and that you hate him
because you love him?
I just did.
did he care?
probably not.
have you ever had people you love and trust
tell you so many times that you are a failure
and that you lie, steal, and cheat
and that you are screwing yourself,
that you actually started to believe them?
I almost did.
but then have you realized that the biggest lie of all
was the so-called 'truth'
coming from the gaping hole of blah on your parents' faces?
have you ever spent
the first eleven years of your life
being criticized so much
that you actually gained
a natural immunity to criticism?
I went through it.
have you ever had
not a single friend in the world
at a young age
and turned to your parents for
actual human compassion and love,
and been turned down?
I have . . . many times.
have you ever realized
that there is no definition of normal.
that the only words able to describe the term normal
are as follows:
normal, in the eyes of a human,
is when another person does the same thing

using similar actions
compared to the original person.
I do and think things in very different ways
than other people do.
therefore, I am weird, messed up, psychotic, crazy, unusual, whatever,
from those people's perspectives,
Aren't I?
do my parents understand that?
yeah, right.
do my parents understand
that I can truly only be
who I truly am,
and no other?
yeah, right.
they believe that if I am
accused of doing something wrong,
something I did not do,
I must act very remorseful and sorry
for what I 'did'.

have you ever gotten
pissed off at your father so many times
that you lose count after bottling up your anger
for seven years straight?
I am.
have you ever blown up at your father
when he finally pushes you way too far over that eccentric edge?
I just did.
have your parents ever asked you
if you wanted to leave the family,
for good?
they have, so many times that I've lost count.
have you ever tried to be artistic?
have your parents ever told you
that your artistic ability was making you
look like a liar, cheater, and a stealer?

I have, numerous times.
have you ever been
in such an emotional and mental state
of confusion. And seconds later your parents
act as though they are supreme?
that they are the ones whose reputations
have been tarnished?
not even!
that their reputations have been scuffed,
lightly touched, fluttered?
my parents have . . . way too many times.
have your parents ever not cared
about the fact that your reputation
has been thrown away, mauled, raped, killed,
deemed non-existent?
my parents don't care.
have you ever kept a secret
from your parents so well
that when the school asks about it,
your parents deny it,
then chastise you
for making them look stupid?
and you have to grit your teeth
in order to keep yourself from exploding
at your parents and telling them everything?
I've been keeping it up
for almost two years.
and I'm damn good at it.
have you ever worked your ass off in school
trying your all to do your best?
and have your parents told you,
as if it's the total truth,
that what you're doing
is the most un-godly act
that has ever been done,
every single night?

my parents have, every single night.
does it feel as if anyone cares?
Have you ever believed
That you shouldn't act differently
Around different people?
Have you ever believed in something greater?
(in yourself?)
Have you ever?

THE LULL OF THE WAVE

and flow,
 the mighty ocean,
through and through.
Plow through everything
that stands in your way.
The powerful one must be Him
to drive the force
of the mighty ocean.
Ho! There is only one fault
in Him who is most powerful:
the Lull of the Wave.

It comes in unexpected,
even He cannot foresee it.
It gives the space for evils
that have been forgotten to set in, once again.
It is a time in which all should be
about as careful as they can.
For without care,
I warn you,
come the evils that you once conquered.
I, myself,
would not want to have to
conquer them once again.

WINDOWS TO YOUR SOUL
⚘

If your eyes are the windows to your soul,
Then what are your eyelids supposed to be?
And if your eyes are the windows to your
Soul, then what are your tears supposed to be?
And if your eyes are the windows to your
Soul, then what are your eyelashes supposed
To be? And if your eyes are the windows
To your soul, then what are your eyebrows sup-
Posed to be? And if your eyes are the win-
Dows to your soul, then where is the door
To your soul supposed to be? And if your eyes
Are the windows to your soul, then what is
Your soul?

WHILE I WAIT
⚘

So much depends upon
A single person,
Who everyone else is
Waiting on.
Waiting on the one,
And makes him sweat.

⚘

"For he who takes the time to dwell on his past does so by wasting
the present as well as all opportunities along the way."

⚘

MIRRORS
✣

Everyone has a
Bad side.
It just depends on when and where
It shows itself.

SRORRIM
✣

a sah enoyrevE
.edis daB
erehw dna nehw no sdneped tsuj tI
flesti swohs tI

༄

"On every occasion that opportunity knocks, answer.
Answer no matter how impossible or improbable the feats seem to be,
for that which does not kill you, makes you that much stronger."

༄

SO MUCH
✣

So much depends upon
Something.
So much depends upon
Everything.
So much depends upon
Me.
So much depends upon
So little.

I AM
⚜

a lover.
I am . . .
A boxer
A pacifist.
I am . . .
A baseball player.
A hockey player.
I am . . .
A dreamer.
A deep sleeper.
I am . . .
Kind.
Gentle.
Harsh.
Both.
Neither.
Optimistic.
I am . . .
Funny . . . I think.
Willing to get down and dirty.
I am . . .
Relaxed.
I am . . .
Genuine,
Original.
I am . . .
Neither an introvert
Nor an extrovert.
I am . . .
Tall,
And short.
Fat,
And skinny.

I am . . .
Artistic.
Athletic.
I am . . .
A man,
A boy,
A young man,
A baby.
I am . . .
A child . . .
At heart.
I am . . .
Black.
White.
I am . . .
Purposeful,
And purposeless.
I am . . .
Bold.
Laid back.
Pointless.
With merit,
And without merit.
I am . . .
Someone who has something good to say.
Someone who has nothing to say at all.
I am . . .
Without wisdom.
With wisdom.
I am . . .
Without power over myself.
With power over myself.
Without power over others.
With power over others,
Then without power over others
All over again.

I am . . .
Out of control.
In control.
Spiraling upward.
Spiraling downward.
Then spiraling downward
All over again.
Stopped.
I am . . .
Falling.
Flying.
Doing nothing.
I am . . .
Doing everything . . .
EVERYTHING!
I am . . .
Fighting for nothing,
Then,
Fighting for everything.
I am . . .
Fighting for a cause
With all my heart,
Then,
Being told that my cause was a joke.
I am . . .
Not a loser
Or a winner.
I am . . .
Beauty.
Ugliness.
I am . . .
Faithful.
Generous.
Colorful.
I am . . .
Slow,

And fast.
I am . . .
Always in control
Of my own destiny.
Yet,
Seem never to be
In control
Of my own destiny.
I am . . .
Different . . .
Always different,
And strangely,
Always the same.
Yet,
Always different.
I am . . .

My
Own
Self

I am . . .
Lonely.
I am . . .
Me.
I am . . .
An I.
I am not
A person that hates.

༈

"I am not in need of the comfort of having the fake answers to the unanswerable questions given to me in the form of believing in a higher power."

༈

HER SMILE HOLDS ME IN CAPTIVITY

Her smile holds me in captivity.
She dresses like no other,
As if she doesn't care at all.
Yet, she cares a great deal.
She is one of the few who have a personality,
At least where I come from.
She is frail, yet
So strong.
She is obvious, yet,
So perplexing.
She is strong, yet,
So gentle.
She is beautiful.
She is   funny.
She is   everything.
Smart.
Witty.
Energetic.
Giving.
Caring.
Loving.
Polite.
And more:
Everything I dreamed of . . .

Everything.

Her laugh holds me . . .
Her voice, so melodious, holds me paralyzed . . .
Her thoughts, so mysterious, hold me perplexed...
Her actions hold me perplexed even more so . . .
Her body holds me stunned . . .
Her face holds me mesmerized . . .

Her eyes hold me waiting . . .
Her smile holds me
In captivity.
But . . .*

ISN'T IT NOT?

❧

A wisdom is not
Held in a box,
But most think of it
As palpable.
Windows are on the walls of the box
That keeps us
In.
What is outside the box
Is wisdom.
In a sense,
The situation is not unlike our universe.
What is in space is us.
What is
Where and when space ends?
Imagination.

LOOKING OUT OF A BUS WINDOW
꙰

I see many new things,
Both young and old,
New and used,
Shiny, rusty, dirty, and clean
I see many new things,
Colors,
Bright, dull, fascinating, boring,
Eye-catching, warm, inviting,
Ominous, ordinary, out of the ordinary.
I see many new things,
Rough, smooth,
Happy, sad, joyful, flowing,
And empty.
I see things move in speed.
In higher speeds.
In higher speeds yet!
In all speeds, for that matter!
But, in reality,
If there is such a thing,
I am the one that is moving,
And yet, am not moving.
I guess perspective has a say in things.
Would you like to know
What I think?
Ha!
What I think . . .
I think I think too much.
I also think that I wish
That more people would stop
To look around themselves more often.
That more people would stop
And think about what other people are
Thinking about more often.

That more people would stop
And think about the hardships
That others have gone through more often.
That more people would stop
And imagine what it would look like
Outside of themselves more often.
That more people would stop
And try to see things from other's perspectives.

CHAPTER 2

UNSHELTERED

A DAY IN THE LIFE OF MY SHOE
✵

Well, it wasn't mine in the first place,
But this is how it goes:
It started out in the store,
The salesperson told me
That it was for sale.
I was happy because I liked the shoe, too.
So I paid the lady at the cash register,
In cash, how much the shoe was worth,
And left with the shoe on.

Now think about how every morning I wake up,
And put it on,
Then tie it up.
Some days I spill stuff on it,
And some days I don't.
Some days I step in poop,
And some days I don't.
Some days I run,
And some days I don't.
Some days I step in gum,
But most days I don't.

But think about how it feels
To be abused every single day.
Think about how it would feel
To be abused every day.

CAGED

❄

Here I am,
Caged in a box.
Nobody knows who I am or where I'm from.
All I am is who I am,
For I am somebody after all, . . .
Aren't I?

SO HIGH

❄

It is Me, the almighty,
sitting on the top of my mountain.
I can make this mountain bigger
if I wanted to.
And I could make you smaller, too.
i feel so good on My mountain top,
But wait . . .
what's this?
I've made you all so small.
I bet you all feel so bad,
When I'm up here and all.
even worse, I've just realized,
They all don't care or see me
way up here on my mountain top and all.
They all don't see
that I am really upside-down,
And spiraling downwards,
and that I cannot stop.

WHY LIVE?

✻

I'll answer that . . .
                    Because when one morning
you wake up and realize that life sucks, you
have realized the truth that there are so ma-
ny bad things in the world like pollution,
drunk driving, murder, rape, the killing of
animals, lies, and that there is nothing
to do in life, and that you are worth no-
thing, and that you won't accomplish any-
thing because your life is a blink of an
eye. Well, I'll tell you why you should live . . . be-
cause when one morning you wake up and think
you realize that life sucks, and you think that
you have realized the ultimate truth that
there are so many bad things in the world
like pollution, drunk driving, murder, rape,
the killing of animals, the cutting
down of rainforests, lies, and that there is
nothing really to do in life, and you
think that you are worth nothing, and that you
won't accomplish anything because your
life is a blink of an eye, you have to
triumph over all of those things in or-
der to get to the very next day.

UNTITLED POEM #0

Never will I experience what I
wish that I could experience. She coughs
towards my direction. Does she wish I go
to hell? Then if she wishes that on me,
then I will go away to hell haste when
she wishes it be so. Only when the
clock strikes midnight, you wish death upon me.
Stare at you, I will not do, for you wish
me not. Your anger wants me to fight hard!
. . . But my sadness wants me to cry, for you
wish for nothing but what shall be done and
in minutes are many days when I'm not
around you. You say that you know that I
don't know myself at all. And I repent.

UNTITLED POEM #1

The heavens stood still,
And nobody cared,
Except for one little boy,
Who just sat and stared
While the heavens stood still.

UNTITLED POEM #3

and the last gleaming rays of the sun's final
emitions hit the summits of all the
mountain tops, we all stared in
silence as the stars shone to
us in all their glory how
beautiful nature can be
without saying a
word.

ROCK MOUNTAIN

So much depends upon the Rock Mountain,
It stands so proud and tall. And yet, so hum-
Ble. It gives way for nothing, nothing at
All. It is the smartest one of its kind.
It does its work behind the scenes, yet it
Has no emotions. It wants to feel, and
Everyone sees that, yet it is too proud
And tall to do so. It is a para-
Dox, for it does not know what to do.

SOLO

Here I am in my imaginary box,
Not a soul in sight.
Here I am in the middle of the desert,
In my imaginary box,
They come and go with wood, water, and toilet paper,
And are gone without a word.
Here I am,
All alone,
Not a soul in sight.
Maybe they won't forget me . . .
Maybe.

FLOATING FREELY

Floating freely,
High and proud,
Totally oblivious
That this heavenly ride
Will not last.

THE CENTER
�֎

Have you ever wondered what it feels like
To die? It doesn't feel like anything
Because death doesn't feel. It just is. The
Last thing you want is to die. That is why
Life is like a labyrinth: the idea
Is not to get to the end, but to take
Your time in getting there.

LOOKING BACK
✳

Look back
Upon that world
That seems so distant
From this world.
It seems so small,
So unhealthy and sick.
It seems so sad,
So horribly depressing.
It seems so twisted,
So happily aggravating.
I took away
So many new skills.
I seem as though
I'm a totally new person.
But when looking back
I can see
How horribly disgusting
And easily maddening

And forgivingly torturing
It really was.

Somehow, I made it through.
Somehow, I am here at home, too.
Somehow, I am not without you.
But I cannot help
Looking back
At that simple seven weeks
That changed my life.
At that simple seven weeks
That changed my life.

So many things that
I went through.
So many times that
I cried the night through.
So many times that
I thought of home and you.
So many times that
I thought to be sheltered.
And all I could do
Was nothing at all.
Look back
At that simple seven weeks
And it changed my life.

So many things.

CHAPTER 3

ARMAGEDDON

CAGED IN A BOX
❄

caged in a box,
a sad little boy sits,
too afraid to come out of the box
that cages him so easily in.
a red bath towel
sits alone,
all by itself,
crying in its own little individual corner.
the silhouette in the windowsill
is all that is left of the
rich little boy
that lived in the house,
caged in himself,
staring in himself.
I'll never let you go,
when the moon sets
and the sun rises
never again.
God is real and omnipresent,
I think not.
everything
will be nothing; taken away
from me;
to   me;
to be given back.
and when it all comes down,
the snow starts falling,
and the necklace moves around some,
as he reminds me that there is another.
random thought
processed through random minds
through and throughout empty space
that is full of empty things that are

full of random thoughts
given to be taken away by
things being allowed in
places they shouldn't.

And the   snow stopped falling.

IN THE MIDDLE OF THE BEGINNING
OF A NEW WORLD
❊

Have you ever experienced the fear
of being in the middle of the be-
ginning of a new world? Have you ever
felt the nervousness of starting out blind,
all by yourself? Have you ever gone through
the pain of meeting new people? Starting
anew is simply hard to do. It feels
simple until you get to the begin-
ning, and you are at the starting line; then
you start to shake. Your throat ties up, like your
heart is in your throat. Your stomach ties up
in knots. When you walk towards the new, your legs
shake uncontrollably. When it finally
happens, you begin to realize that it's
going to be okay.

PLAYING GOD
✳

is something not to do.
if everyone, all of a sudden,
was no different from anyone else,
then who would you be?
i don't have a clue.
you tell me.
i'm talking to you, scientists!
if you even think of creating a catalog
of some sorts
for what a couples' baby could be,
then fine.
humanity will pay the price.
it'll only be the end of the human race.
no big deal!
i can understand
getting rid of every genetic disease,
but to give parents a choice
of what their baby could be,
it would be the end of the world . . .
Period.
it would be like playing *The Sims* computer game,
except SO much more detailed . . .
it would be playing God.

CAGED INNOCENCE
⚜

And unaware of all things, she is,
Being blissful to all the things
As her miserable life passes her right on by.
And miserably beautiful it is,
While she sits there unaware,
Of all the things that should be thought of
Very much more carefully.
The toys that live inside with her
Only show that she'll be there for a time
That can't be measured in a thoughtful or happy way.
The cage is still there, and dirty it is,
But she's being true to her bliss.
And she cackles like no tomorrow,
Day in and day out, of course.
The juice sits there,
Not being noticed,
She was never taught to sing,
And probably never will be taught
By anyone who cares.
Slanted are the lovely things,
And of course, they always will be,
For the lovely things are only as lovely
As the cage will ever be.
And don't you wish, that she'd be free
Someday when the skies are blue?
Wishing that, I am; I did;
And of course, I still do.
But think about it logically,
She wouldn't make it outside,
Because her wings wouldn't be used to it,
And they wouldn't be fit at all.
Frayed, the edges will be, when time takes it's toll,
But she'll still be there,
For gone is her soul.

و~

"In this day and age, to hate is a sin. In this day and age,
the word 'hate' is uttered continuously, without a second thought."

و~

BITTERSWEET

Bittersweet poetry
would describe my life perfectly,
but only would it describe my life
until it reached the constrictions of
the English language.

It is bittersweet for it always ends in tragedy.

Bittersweet movies
would explain my life perfectly,
but only would they explain my life
until they reached the constrictions of
our modern technology.

It is bittersweet for it always ends in tragedy.

Bittersweet stories
would depict my life perfectly,
but only would they depict my life
until they reached the constrictions of
the English language.

It is bittersweet for it always ends in tragedy.

Bittersweet life
would unfold my life perfectly,
until it reached the constrictions of
my passing on to another place.

Love is bittersweet for it always ends in

tragedy.

⚘

"Life sucks. And sometimes life is full of a thousand problems that are the
size of Texas, while you are just the size of an ant.

Deal with it."

⚘

FEELING BLUE

Everything stops
when something's wrong,
I don't want to do
anything at all.
Slowly, I move,
down the barren hall,
To find a place
to rest my haggard soul.
A note is resting
peacefully in my hand,
It validates my feelings
with the ink of dirty blood.
She says that there is
but one thing to do.

She gives me the painkillers,
and I choke them down,
Trying my best to forget the taste
of all my sickened loneliness.
And as I walk back down the hall,
which I've walked so many times,
I start to wonder if this will ever end.
and I open my door,
And take back my seat,
all while still feeling blue.

LIFE IS A BLINK OF AN EYE
❊

Freedom!
Serenity!
Purity!

Prancing around the world,
Unheeded!
Untainted!

Free!

Life is mine!

I am invincible!

Free!
Free!!
Free!!!

Burdenless!
Painless!
Free as a bird!

Prancing around the world,
Untouched!
Pure!

Free!

Held down by nothing!
Vroom . . . vroom!
VROOM . . . VROOM!!

Free!
Thwump, THWUMP!

. . .

. . . .

. . . .

(The life, and death, of a fawn)

life is short.

FIRE DRILL
❊

Did you ever wonder why, when officials say, 'please walk quickly and quietly to the nearest available exit,' not one single person walks quickly or quietly, or walks at all?

Running
through the hallways,
don't know what to do,
try to
scream,
but nothing comes out.
I
Panic
when the threat of
Death
is imminent.
my body starts to give out. I

fall
onto my face,
smashing
my nose. It would be so
Sad
to watch my fallen body,
writhe
on the bloody ground,
unable to save myself.

And suddenly,
The blackness envelops me like a warm blanket.

THE CEILING FAN

Goes round and round.
The clock goes round and round.
The color red
Is unbearable.
Blue, on all sides, does
Nothing to comfort me
While white is
Stepped on more
And more,
Becoming less white with every step.
Green seems to be present
Nevermore.
Black is rushing
In.
S'funny,
I thought I was

Invincible.
I knew I was
Indestructible.
Boy,
Was I
Wrong.
The Ceiling Fan
Goes round and round.
One push
Of one button,
And everything

Stops

No matter how important.
But the Ceiling Fan
Goes round and round.

WHERE AM I?
❧

It's hot.
And oh-so-hot!
Why is it so dark?
I feel so scared.
I feel more lonely
Than I ever have in
My entire life.
Is this hell?
Why is it hot, but wet?
Oh, please, God, tell me,
Why?
Why?
Why does this have to happen to me?
Is it my fault?
Have I disgraced myself?
Have I disgraced my family or friends?
Where did I go wrong?
So terribly wrong?

I lift my head up heavily,
And still,
As always,
I have been lying
On my bed with my face
In my pillow.
And then it hits me.

TRAGEDY STRIKES

Ka-blam!
And it ends

Bam!
     The end.

 Adios, Tonto,
And the horse you rode in on, too.
Ain't gonna be any survivors.
S'like an A-bomb went off
Inside my head.
S'like a bullet
Went through my heart.
S'like I was punched
In my stomach.

 Boom!
       Finito.

 Fwap!
     TKO.
          Gameover.

 S'like my eyes are going to burn up.
S'like a meteor went through my heart.
S'like a volcano erupted
In my stomach,
And took a piece of my heart
Along with it.
Then every single thing
Slowed down
All the way to a
Stop.

 Ka-blam!
And it ends.

THE OMINOUS 'THEY'

※

While lying in my nice and pretty bed,
I wonder why I have not really read
Of thé misfortunes of my dearest friend,
Who has maný wounds to which he must tend.
Some information, is what I must lend,
To thé man that I call my dearest friend.
As thé confídant, I need not pretend.
While lying in my dank and dusty bed,
Like most peoplé, I do frequéntly tend
To drift off into á mindless deep énd.
And as my eyes roll back into my head,
I think about last night's events, and dread;
Which gives my idle dreary sleeping mind
Something to dream of, of a different kind.

While lying in my cómfortáble bed
I hear a knock coming from my windów,
Which brings to the windów my tired head.
At thé windów, looking at thé tree, "Oh,
I hope those shadows are away today."
Forever still, my fear will always be
At night when the shadows won't go away;
Hey, how'd he get all the way up that tree?
I open thé windów, his eyes are glazed,
His face says to me that something's to fear.
He says to be ready to be amazed,
I feel the evil ones that are so near.
For I have no idea what my friend thinks.
And I do know if my friend is jínxed.

Looking towards hís face, he seems confident,
But there seems to be something in his face,

That just isn't in place, that doesn't sink.
Something to hide, he might have . . . it's disgrace,
I think. My mind is floating on cloud nine,
For my friend and confidant trusts me still,
'Cause he knows when he's with me, he'll be fine,
When I'm the confidant, I know I will
Be truthful to my friend until the end,
And tó listén with án unbiased mind.
He is the man that I'll alwáys defend,
And that a lie from me, he will not find.
True, I'd like my friend to be there for me,
But I know there are places he needs be.

When I am áloft, cóvered bý darknéss,
With mý friend, I reallý start tó get át
The point where I consider, and could miss
All the excitement of all this and that.
My móre horríble emotions are when
I start to want more information on
My confidant and closest, dearest friend.
I think of the giant weight Í bear ón
My shoulders, and I feel like atlas feels,
When he holds up the world with all his might.
Then I start to imagine how it'd feel
To áway things I keep with all my might.
But the real fear for me that is so great,
Is that my confidant is not so great.

And worst of all's when sorrow makes a cut.
My friend, I feel bad for alwáys when he
Tells me of all those things, that they have cut
My heart in half, will ever make him free.
Now, when you are a strolling or walking,
Have you evér had á twinge of the thought
That somewhere in the night, someone's watchíng?
And is it not scary that you've been brought

To á point where you can't go out at night?
And is it not really upsetting when
You feel as if paranoid you just might
Be? And your mind will be odd now and then.
And is it not scarý that your thinkíng
Shadows, that they'll be áfter you comíng?

As we walk in the blackness of a hall,
Not íncludíng my good friend béhind me,
I do not feel verý aloné at all,
My mind says quick to me that I should flee.
A bigger problem in a deeper sense
Might be a thing my friend probábly has.
And as we're walking over a small fence,
I ask again, and he says, "because . . ." as
We're walking down the slippery stairs once more,
I feel them from a place I know not true.
The light switch I am turning on once more.
Stop, I so wish that those shadows would do.
I feel their eyes bearíng down on my back,
And I wished that running, I did not lack.

My friend says forcefullý, "Stop, confidant,"
I question, "What is your lengthý businéss,
To know what it is, ís something I want."
"Oh, I have something that I must confess,"
I look at shadows that I cannot see,
My friend says, likely, he is, to defy
"I see the shadows, my big problem be,"
and as I think what he has said's a lie,
and as I am the confidant to him,
and to be my own confidant he tries,
I look around and hear an off-tune hymn,
And see my life flash quick before my eyes.
And I remember staring at the tree,
As those dark shadows jump right out at me.

In deep cold sweat, I do wake lying in,
"Wow, last night was one of those dreams I've had!
I hope that I won't have that dream again!"
And as I think something will happen bad,
I see my friend dear júst lýing right there,
Staríng right at me with a glare emptý.
A note is posted on his chest, aware
He is, that a confidant he's of me.
The note also said that he was my friend
And that his confídant, I surely was.
It said when talked to, he did not pretend.
It said that told to lie, he really was
By those shadows, but he thought to defy
Myself, and fight the shadows, he did try.

CHAPTER 4

REBIRTH

A BOAT WITH MANY HOLES TO BE PATCHED
✳

I have lived many a year
Where my boat has sunk so near . . .
But every time I've taken my hammer and nail
And put a hole in my boat,
Common sense, I've had enough,
To patch them up myself, though tough.
But as many know,
There are only so many times that a patch can be put
On a wound of the hull of a boat.
So, once on a morning of sweet dewdrops,
With many a song being sung
But the beautiful birds in the lofty treetops,
My little study boat
(Which does have many an unsturdy thing about it!)
wasn't so sturdy anymore,
as it sank down into the sea,
not to be seen by anyone or me.

THAT MYSTERIOUS GIRL
❊

Every single day of mine
She passes me in our dreary hall.
And even though she is so fine,
She perplexes my racing mind and all!
I don't know what,
And surely not how,
To do anything about it!
What shall I do?
What shall I do?
So calm and tranquil over here,
And hyper over there!
Perplexing me left and right, up and down.
Go back to where you came from,
And leave my poor, lonely heart alone!
Through and throughout the days and the nights,
I can't stop thinking about you and of you!
You confound my mind to the deepest extent!
I can't forget!
And can't unremember
All you smiles,
And all of your laughs,
And all of your hellos,
And all of the wonderful things you've said!
I wish they'd all go away
As quickly and as sweetly
As they came in!
So mysterious you are being to me,
To love you, as far as I can see,
Is the only way for me to be free!

OUR OWN

Have you ever had the feeling
That you already knew something,
But you've never heard it before?
You're absolutely right! In a sense!
For all you know of anything,
Really is precisely everything,
If you know anything at all!
Now, this is only my knowing,
And no one else's at all,
For no one seems to know but me!
All of all and every little thing
That stands in between all things,
Is known to you and to me!
Even the dumb ones know it all,
They just can't remember anything.
So call all knowledge your own,
For I do,
So that surely makes all things known
Our Own, and nothing more and nothing unknown!

SCRAPS

✳

Doesn't anyone realize
That things left behind
Are really good,
Not at all worthless,
At least when put together.

Happily I live
With all the things
That are left behind
By others with no care.
And I feel for all the chaps
Who say they don't need all their scraps.

UNTITLED POEM #7

✳

If, one day, you have some time,
Look through a hole,
And what will you see . . .
A world that's full of possibility!
And a chime,
To make a goal,
It is time.
Now, on we go!

THE BULLY

Big and tall he stood there,
right in front of me.
His muscles bulging,
his shirt ripping,
As he breathed right down on me.
his mouth was yelling,
Or so it seemed,
because I wasn't listening.
I was too busy
with my own thoughts,
Busying themselves about him.
one said run,
The other said fight,
and the little one said to talk it out.
I decided on all three,
but a movement from me,
No one could see,
for my body had frozen on me.

THE COMMANDER, OUR GODLY "SAVIOR"

❃

The stroll down the leisurely pathway was taken,
careful to disturb nothing at all . . .
Look!
A Savior,
on high!
Comes on bold wings with His broad horse,
here to make the Right Decisions.
Well, He has saved us all.
Day in, day out,
given to us is all we want,
and then some.
Wow, life is too perfect.
          Did we say that?
               We hope not!
Too late!
For now we have gone against the . . . "How, will
she none?" The Commander, Our Godly "Savior" bellows,
"Doth she not give us thanks,
Is she not proud?
Doth she not count her blessings,
Unworthy as she is, that we have
Wrought so worthy ('Ha!') a gentleman
To be her bride?" And
bellow your great "Commander, Your Godly "Savior,"
for It, or He, or
Whatever,
shall bellow all It, or He, or Whatever, wants,
for It is full of hot air,
and zoning out occurs when
hot air is blown in
the faces of the young and
love-struck and pure.

Go through the motions,
It does,
of an enraged father.
Obvious, it really is,
for I have seen it
a thousand times too many.
But, all mistakes,
in fathers' eyes, at least,
must be learned from,
or else they, too, will be
just mistakes. Too bad
that nobody here learns from the mistake
of believing in Their Commander, Their Godly "Savior."

Taken away
All must be
Before punishment
Takes care of the rest of us

So throw a high pitched scream,
or belt out a deep, menacing yell,
throw your beautifully ugly temper-tantrums,
but get up and wipe away
your tears anyway,
and take the brutal punishment that
you so deserve, but never,
Ever,
try to defy
Our Commander, Our Godly "Savior."

THINGS AT NIGHT
❊

Things at night
Are scary,
But the things at day
Are scarier than any of anyone could imagine.
They make your hair stand on end
And do things to your helpless mind
That one thinks will not mend.
I think that you will find
Things in the day of a scarier kind!
They don't hide in closets
Or in your drawers
Or under your bed!
They walk around hidden by nothing,
For they can't be found by naked eyeing!

WHAT I LOVE
❊

What I love to see,
Walking down the hall,
Of a high school that's near me,
Are many not so dreary faces,
Staring back at me.
To look in all their growing faces
Is so lovely for me
And to see all the great things
That might come to be.
I love to see in all the faces
The possibility of the idea to be free,

But only are the grime ones,
And they know where they'll be,
Knowing who they are,
What I love most about them
Is that they think they know it all.

ENDS OF ALL AND EVEN SO
※

Angered through and through
My bitter soul.
To the distant ends of it, even!
(If you can say that there are ends to a soul)
Wow! That felt good!
To throw things across the room,
But it doesn't quench my thirst for blood,
Which comes whistling softly down the stairs,
Passing me by even softer so;
And I should be putting my shoes on now.
Yeah   in a shoulda, coulda, woulda world
Maybe!
In earnest
Jumping and banging
And jumping to conclusions
But in the end,
It's all the same.
Hey, what's the difference?
But the check is in the mail,
And I've already been disconnected,
So tell me,
Who's side am I supposed to be on now?
When the bridge collapses

And the big man falls
Through the ice
And into the even icier water,
Who is supposed to be drowning now?
And when my heart
Crosses the white line
To the other side of the way,
Who's laughing now?
Sorry . . . no through
Speed limit, buddy . . .
But who thought that that was going to happen, anyway?
No chance there will be a Freedom!
That's like the sun setting in the A.M. to me.

A THOUSAND GLASSES

✣

I wish, I wish, I wish,
That I could see through
Your thousand glasses,
As I can see through mine.
I'd have to know you really well,
To know what color they all are.

I hope, I hope, I hope,
That I could feel the way you feel
Through your thousand glasses
As I feel all the time through mine.
I'd have to know you really well,
To know exactly what shades they all are.

HATEFUL LOVE OF A TIME

Her smile is so beautiful
and yet I hate her so,
I wish she wouldn't be there
when I look around the way.
Leave me be!
and hold him tight!
For an idiot he may be,
but I hope he keeps you warm at night,
And I wish you'd do the same for me.
and I wish! That I could find another
That cared for me as much
as I cared for you
Once upon a time.
long ago, it was all so good
When all was so innocent,
and everything was so pure and flawless,
And I could be myself with you.
and the walls are crumbling,
My hold ring falling off my empty finger,
as the love turns bittersweet
While the peacekeeper throws away his keys.

off, my emotions had started to flake
And then and now, my hands start to shake.

UNTITLED POEM #8
⚘

At the end of all days and things and wings
There begins a new beginning
That is so old it has a beard
That hangs way down to the ground.

At the end of all days and things and wings
There begins a new ending.
The same as before
That is so young that all it has
Is a wisp of golden hair atop its crown.

At the end of all days and things and wings
There begins a new middle
That is so in the middle
That it is neither balding
Nor growing hair anew.

At the end of all days and things and wings
There begins all days and things and wings between
The new beginnings, new endings,
And, of course, the new middles.

And at the end,
All things begin
While all the others pause to watch.

CHAPTER 5

CHANGED TIMES

POOLSIDE

❦

All the scantily-clad people
Flex their bodies
In hope of mastering the art of courtship
Or hope to get lucky.
And they all douse themselves with oil
And water and products bad for the body
Or lounge in recliners or swim in the grasses
In front of the ant-trodden pool.
Or they dawn shirts or towels
As they eat to their heart's content.
And then some.
Only the men who don't come miss out
As well as the few who miss out anyway.

FROM BEHIND

Why do the birds fly away so readily
When I walk not even too near?
I'd like to know
Why they go
And come again
Like the clouds and the wind
On a night like this morning.
Surely it isn't a hormone
That makes them hate me so!
Maybe it's an impurity
In my heart or in my soul.
I hope it's not,
For if it was,
Then there's something wrong with me.

UP OR DOWN

As I stood in front of an elevator in my hotel,
I contemplated the deep question:
Should I go up or should I stay?
Should I go left or right, I may?
Or should I sit and wallow
In my self-pity
And yawn here
Wondering where to go in my life?
So I got in.

꙳

"Chaos in confined spaces is not the most comfortable experiences."

꙳

꙳

"How could it be so hard to meet new people in a
new place when you're all alone?"

꙳

ASHLEY
꙳

I wish I wish I wish I wish
That I had the pleasure
To meet you.
You seem so nice,
I almost wish
That I met you twice.
But sadly clouds will cover the sky
When you pass me on by.
I hate grass,
Because that's what I stood on
When you walked on through my sky.

MINDS INFLUENCED BY SOCIETY
AND THE PAST
❧

The little boy
On the nice lady's back
Points to me and says "Black,"
And I say, "White," and point
To my skin.
He leaves his nice mother's back,
Walks over to me,
And points to my shirt,
And says, "Black,"
And I say, "Exactly."
Then he goes back
And gets on his nice mother's back,
And yells shrilly and points
To the deep end of the pool,
"Giddy-up!"
and rides away into the blue.

UNTITLED POEM #28
❧

All the people
I know so well,
And yet know so little,
Look me in the eyes.
But why can they only
Hold my gaze for a moment,
Until they can't hold
Any more?

A blob on the floor,
One sitting in a chair,
And a daffodil sitting lonely
On a desk.
It is so wonderful
And so beautiful
And so magnificent,
But still is all alone.
So frail it sits,
So strong it means to me.

UNTITLED POEM #29

What   I love
Will never be
And will never be the same to me.
My anger's shot
And my sadness is too sad
To be mad or sad about it.
What you love
Will never stay
The way you always want it to be.
And what you love
Is taken from you
Without a word of anything.

My love's been taken
By someone nameless,
Merely doing his job.
What's worse is that
When it rains milk,
It pours sour.

UNTITLED POEM #30
✤

I wish that I
Was not right here
But instead,
Somewhere near.
But not here,
You must see,
I hate it so,
Don't you see,
I can't stand the words
You cast down dark upon me.

JIGGLE JIGGLE
✤

Too bad,
I really am sorry,
But jiggling your plastic
And smiling your seductive silicone at me
Just won't work like it used to.
I now own something that is not bought,
I have dignity,
Which is something your plastic parts
Can't give you.

NIXING OF IMPORTANT THINGS

I wish I wish I wish
That I could bring it back
From wherever it is now.
For wherever that is,
I'll tell you this
Is somewhere not to be found.

I wish I wish
That it was fixed
For today and not later on.
That it stayed here,
And I had no fear
That it might not come at all.

I wish
That all things were beautiful,
And important things weren't needed;
Especially one so morbid;
Such as this one,
Which is happening not now,
But never again.

"Wounds will heal in time, and yes, so will broken hearts, but right now,
the pain is real, and it's not going away."

SOMETHING SPECIAL

✼

Just because it's broken
Doesn't mean that it's gone for good
Or even broken for good.
It's only broken at the moment.
But, it's broken at the moment,
But that's enough to break other things, too.
Other things were broken,
And now are mended,
And others are broken for good.
But things not fully broken
Can be mended in time
To come out better than before.
Let us all hope so.

SLIGHTLY INFATUATED

(To A Girl I Got to Know During the Summer of 2001, Katheryn French)

✼

VERSE I

Tie a bed onto my car
I have a feeling that we'll go far
And I
Won't forget.

Drop an anvil on my feet
I won't forget when we did meet
And I
Can't be mean.

CHORUS
My training wheels have got to fall
Out to you I have to call
That I
Love you.

VERSE II
A sideways cross looks hard at me
When you're mean I want to flee
And I
Come right back.

Trees may die and pigs may fly
I loved you the night I wore a tie
And I
Want you here.

CHORUS
My training wheels have got to fall
Out to you I have to call
That I
Love you.

VERSE III
I can taste these lands of waste
If you turn away it's what I'd face
And I
Will set you free.

Trains go by, I don't know why
If pain was coming, for you I'd die
And I
Saw you there.

BRIDGE
A guy once told me so:
A path life, love will go.
And through it two will sow
The seeds of love and they'll grow

Someday they'll have a lawn to mow
They'll hold hands with two kids in tow
They won't care if the world turns blue
Only that their love is true.

CHORUS

My training wheels have got to fall
Out to you I have to call
That I
Love you.

VERSE IV

Raindrops jumping from the ground
I thank God that you I've found
And I
Dream again.

A shoelace I dream of ties itself
To another like itself
And I
Die dreaming.

CHORUS

My training wheels have got to fall
Out to you I have to call
That I
Love you.

CHORUS

My training wheels have got to fall
Out to you I have to call
That I
Love you.

END (SLOW)

They won't care if the world turns blue
Only that their love is true.

NOT IN THE BACK OF MY MIND

(Also To The Girl I Got to Know During the Summer of 2001, Katheryn French)

⚜

This is real
I cannot deny
The feelings I try to hide.
The present decides the future
Every moment, something changes.
I want to change our destiny.
This is different for me.
Are you going through with this
Because I won't see you again
Tomorrow?
What do you feel?
Explain it here.
You must
For I myself don't trust.
I am at your upper crust,
But I want to java
Your inner core's molten lava.
If you forget about me,
Your cheeks will turn white,
But you won't know why,
Because you won't remember.
But you will remember.
I'm walking away . . .
I'm walking away!
Why am I walking away?
When you walked away,
You didn't look back,
You broke my heart in the process.
Why did you not turn back?
Were you laughing?
Were you crying?
A rose

Means more than prose.
My words won't ever be
Able to describe my
Feelings for you
A stem
Means more than a poem.
A thorn
Means destiny has scorn.
A rose in the mouth of a dove
Means forty years later there is love.
I catch a cold
From the love you threw
At me
And left.
Later

I walked towards your door
In shambles,
Shaking and crying.
All I could manage was,
"I am going to miss you."
French K.F.C.
Is always good to me
Even if it leaves
Every night at three.
Remember all the good times
The good rhymes
The good thyme
Remember the sunshine
The boat's chimes
The hard easy lines.
I love you
You love me
We could have been happy
Your heart was opening
But mine a wide open door

Thank you please, instead
There's got to be more.
I try to forget.
Try to keep a blank face,
Blank mind.
Everything goes blank,
All hope is lost.

And you appear!
The end was near,
But God changed our fate
With three little words
And gave us one more night.
Fate
Is a funny thing
It doesn't make sense
To you or me.
I am free
I feel change
From you to me.
Down to up
A roller coaster
Is the life I lead
In these 9 days.

That smile on your face
Makes me smile brighter.
The way you rub me
Makes my steps lighter.
The way fate works
Makes my heart a fighter.
The clock on the wall
Makes my grip on you tighter.

You are tall,
I am wide.

I am small,
Are you tied?
I look between
My parents mean,
And see something
Palpable flickering.
I look between
Us, you and me
And
What do I see?
Something palpable?
Something unseen?
Something great?
Or something mean?
Something with rhyme?
A chance to dine?
I will tell in time.
You will tell me in time.
But I took your words too lightly
On paper,
Too seriously in mind and soul
And heart.
Those words were super saturated
And totally elated
With meaning beyond belief.
If meant in their silence
To the full potential,
Then I must confide
I flew inside.
Today is the Day of Smiles . . .
No tears.
I don't know anyone as well as you.
Only now does my life feel true.
Why am I saying all this?
I've known you for eight days.

Please, try to write,
It's not that hard.
Just write what you think
Without thinking
Write what you feel . . .
Don't rhyme;
If you don't want to.
If you do,
Do.
If you don't,
Don't.
That goes for everything.

I believe.
In being slightly infatuated
In fate
In the power of request
In help
In God
In you.
In your potential for greatness.
You

I ask for peace,
I get upheaval.
I ask for quiet,
I get medieval.
I ask for love,
I get denied.
I ask for friendship,
I get defied.
I ask for a compliment,
I get a shove.
I ask for nothing,
And I get love.

I am not sure if you like me.
I am not sure why you aren't free.
I am not sure why you try.
I am not sure why you kiss me.
I am not sure if you are tired.
Or if I was somehow suddenly fired.
I am not sure if I am good enough to you.
I am trying hard to be perfectly respectable and nice
And acceptable
And re-memorable
And sociable
And funny
And loud
And quiet
And romantic
And stone-faced
And truth-faced
And erased
And full
And ready
And willing
And able
And fulfilling
And meaningful
And worthwhile
And generous
And purposeful
And soulful
And profound
And smart
And understanding
And nice
And kind
And influential
And helpful
And caring

And loving and perfect.
I AM trying.
Because I care.
You want something,
You got it.
I only want one thing:
To be with you.
That needs a few things . . .
You.
Me.
A connection.
Time.
Freedom.
Trust.
Those we have, right?
I doubt myself way too much.
Maybe you can help me with that.
But that also needs:
Time.
A bond unbreakable
And unbroken.
Us.

I have to stop.
And say thank you.
What you have said
Has meant so much to me.
My heart is free.
I have frolicked many miles . . .
Today really is the day of smiles.
In my mouth are thirty-six tiles,
In my mind are remarkable aisles
Full of memories in vials
That hold my many smiles.
"Smiles,"
That word,

Means so much to me.
It means life,
Liberty in mind, body, soul,
Freedom in mind, body, soul,
Purity in mind, body, soul,
Love in mind, body, soul.

It means happiness,
A little sappiness,
A feelings sea
So new to me,
I'm full of glee,
It won't stop.
It, I can't drop.
Today really is the Day of Smiles!

Who thought the end of summer could hold
Something this timeless and old?
This is a gift.
All of it.
How I got the necklace.
That strange peace.
(I feel a strange happiness at the moment)
finding God.
Talking to Chip Valandra.
Going through that ordeal with Eliza.
Going to Hyde.
Going to Aspen Achievement Academy.
Being short and fat and ugly.
Being a loser,
A jerk,
And an anti-social hothead.
Changing.
Doing the right thing.
Doing the hard easy,
Even when it was very, very, hard.

All in the past, distant.
This is a gift.
The necklace I gave to you.
My Japanese.
Your Japanese.
The poem and the empty pen and the waiter out of nowhere.
The three and a half hours.
The PDA.
Your pink cheeks.
All the metaphors we dwindled on,
Back and forth and left and right.
I appreciate it to the fullest extent
Of my capability.
I am tired, yes,
As are you.
But I am past fear
Regarding you.
I am aware in the present.
I see you,
Even when you are not around.
You may be scared,
But talk, and be free,
And slowly,
It will melt away.
I am still smiling.
I asked for God's help
Five times.
I was answered . . .
Five times
I am still smiling.
There are others
In this vast sea
Surrounding me,
But you believe in me,
What more could I want?
If you feel uncomfortable

With me basically throwing all these poems and songs at you,
Technically a stranger,
Just say so.
What is wrong with me
In your eyes?
What is right with me,
In your eyes?
What am I,
In your eyes?
What am I supposed to do,
In your eyes?

Everything is so symbolic.
I know we're tired
It's so, so true.
I just can't seem
To get rid of you.
Not that I want to . . .
Oh, forget it
I can talk on for miles!
Just tell me a story . . .
Tell me a story of smiles . . .

STRANGERS

❊

You never know
What people grasp
Inside their private lives.
And you never know
What people know
When they pass you on by.

You never know
What potential people hold
When they look you in the eye.
And you never know
What people think
About anything and everything
And I wish that I could find out.

STRANGE
✣

They're not that strange to me and you,
Because they're part of me and you.
But the animals talk about
How we, as humans, have no snout
Or tails or fur or eyes on the side
Or why we walk with our hinds to the side.
They talk amongst themselves about our wars.
They wonder many a thing, from "what are doors,"
To "How those people fly kites."
They wonder why we do such things like
Standing up and singing in front of a mike.
But most of all, they wonder what things

That they should be calling feelings.

THERE'S A ROCK IN MY FOOT

✾

I hate it so much!
It's there
And when asked,
Still will not leave.
And when forced,
Still will not leave.
It hurts enough
To get my attention,
But not enough
To make me give a serious effort
To getting rid of it.
It's just there?

✾

"I ask you not to learn how to deal with your problems.
I ask you to deal with your problems, nothing more. For if you deal with
all your problems, you are not only solving your problems,
but you are learning how to deal with your problems."

✾

SO GROWN UP
✣

My family seems so far away now,
And also seen through a tinted glass plate,
And I wish they wouldn't fade
As the way they are right now.
I'm facing the door
That leads to the horrors of the World,
And I can't help but put my hand on the doorknob.
And all of a sudden,
The music stops
And a long-stemmed pink rose
Hits me in the back of the head
As I step into my life with a smile.

✤

"I bowl. Not really. When I do, I try to aim where I am
going to roll the ball. I get a great score around 60.
I bowl. Not really. When I do, I aim where I am going
to roll the ball. I get a measly score around 200."

✤

UNTITLED POEM #25
❊

Words are such powerful things!
They can be taken in so many ways
That are so very wrong while wings
Carry the only right way that the words of mine
Can be taken by others. Sands are only held aloft
By a thin piece of twine
And only a voice that's soft,
But powerful still,
Can ever quench the people's need
For the blood that they kill.

But let my wings be seen.

UNTITLED POEM #26
❊

what does a picture hold in store
when you take it looking at the sun?
what does it hold
when you've told
that you won't develop it?
what does it hold
but a moment in time,
and they'd be better
if they only cost a dime.

৵

"If you look hard enough, you will find.
If you look, you will never find. If you don't ever look, you will never find.
If you don't look, you will always find.
If you try, you fail. If you try hard, you succeed.
If you don't try, you fail. If you don't try, you succeed."

৵

৵

"What do we need to do to go forward?
Absolutely nothing, because we will go forward anyway."

৵

DARYL

❊

The contrite and pleasant smile
Alighted upon the young man's face
Has a meaning:
Every day, he knows,
He has done his personal best
At his job, and no less.
I would hope and wish that
Everyone would work that way,
And not just the young man
With a smile on his face.

END OF VACATION

❉

I feel as if
I can't express myself any longer.
I feel as if
I can't go on any more.
I'm bruised and battered
And I won't feel flattered
No matter what you say.
I'm soaked to the bone,
I've been taken off my throne
And there's nothing that I own.
I feel like I'm done with this place,
So I'll stop and save face
Because up my sleeve, there is no more ace.

❧

"Nothing is safe no matter how well you hide it, how many times you lock it
up, how far away you keep it, or how far away you keep from it."

❧

SECOND TO LAST

And words can't describe anything for me
When my feelings well up in my throat
When I see my love having a Time of Her Life
Right before my very eyes
While I can actually be a part of that Time,
But never Love
barred by a friend
by hate with a smile.
And love breaks me to tears
In the midst of tearing me
Between three different loves.
I hate it so!
I wish nothing.
I want nothing.
Only what's so
Is what's so
And I hate it
For it will never leave me alone.
And I love you so.
Her smile at me,
and only me,
to me,
all for mine
and the only thing I can call my own,
is so delicate to me.
And tears flow freely
down down down the narrow untrodden pathways
of my heart and soul.
And Teddy Bears
dance in the hallways
Blissfully unaware
that they're standing on railroad tracks.

THE LAST PAGE

I was broken,
But now I am fixed.
I was dead,
But now I am alive.
I was hurt,
But now I am healed.
I was ready,
But now I am tired.
I was lost,
But now am found.
I was willing,
But now I am bored.
I was lost,
But now have a light ahead of me.
I was able,
But now I am unstable.
I have lost,
But now I have regained.
I have wronged,
But now I have righted my wrongs.
I have been wronged,
But now I am righted.
I have begun,
But now I am finished.

CHAPTER 6

THE BUILDUP AND THE BREAKDOWN

MANY MISTAKES
✣

I look back through the years
At all the things I've done
I see the ones that stand alone
Amidst this life of mine
And I see how stupid it was
To deny the very existence
Of things staring me in the face.

FREE FLOWING
✣

Don't look away so quick, please,
    I'll miss your voice,
        Your face
           You.
              And through and throughout my heart, mind and soul
            A being created by you alone
      Runs
                The manifestation of something higher
                Lives in me from you.

Many times I've tried to make it real
    And I have failed.
        But the truth shows itself
           And doesn't like to be found.

I am overwhelmed
    By a flowing sadness
        Washing over my joy,

Turning out the lights on my happiness
Because of all the things between us.

The life within will never leave me,
But will die if not nourished.
That being will drive me
To be with you
Near you
Never without you.

IN THE AIR

You make me so happy
You make me laugh all the time
You make my day brighter
You make my life bearable
You make my burden lighter.
Why am I so sad?

It might be it's over,
It might be what's between us,
It might be the waiting,
Or it could be all the uncertainty.
It might be love
It might be friends
Or it could be nothing at all.
It might be me
It might be you
Or it could be meant to be.
And it still might be nothing at all.
And after I'm finished thinking about it,
Why am I still so sad?

AS OF NOW

I wonder about many things
I wonder about all the possibilities
It makes me sick
To think what could happen
And that it might not be
I wish she would understand
My hand meets hers
She is scared and I can feel it
It melts away
As I caress her
I am scared and she can feel it
It melts away
As she caresses me
We will be scared and we know it
It will melt away
When our hands join together
Once again.
It's a beautiful day.

I WISH I COULD SEE

❋

You seem to have control
But I can see through it.
You seem to have it all set up.
You seem to have it all figured out.
You seem to have the perfect life.
But I can see through it.
I know you don't have a perfect life
Because you are missing me.
I know this because
I'm missing you.

LAZY LOVER

❋

What have I done wrong
To deserve this predicament
That I have so hastily walked into.
I can answer that,
But I don't want to.
I want it,
You want it.
What is so hard?
I can answer that,
But I really don't want to.

IT'S ALL DIFFERENT

And I take a good, hard look
At myself in the mirror,
I ask myself if I know what I am getting myself into.
Yes, I do.
Willingly and without doubt.
With knowledge and without sin.
With love and without looking back.
I am in love.
And I smile.

FLATTERY AND CONFUSION

Life seems so slow
So bland
So boring
Without you here
Without you here to make me smile
And make me laugh all day
I wish that everything was fine
And life went the happy way
And didn't make everything so hard on me
Or anyone, especially you
You bring me so high when I see you
When you're gone
Nothing compares
Life seems so empty
So dull
So dead
Without you here

I hope one day that all will be
Happy and joyful
And good to me
And that I'm able to be good to you
I hope one day that all I know
Would help me be with you
But I know that nothing I do
Will change your decision
Between him and me and you

You fill me full of energy
Full of pep
Full of vigor
Full of emotions I've never felt before
I've never felt more alive
Then when around you

The time that I spend with you
I never want to end
But it flies by so quickly
And you're gone before I know it
Leaving a trail of love and dismay

Life seems so slow
So bland
So boring
Without you here
So make your decision quick
So I can get on with my horrid life,
With or without you
No endings

LEAVE ME ALONE

I don't know what's wrong with me

      And no one seems to care.

I feel so weird inside

       I feel so dry and bare.

I don't know what's wrong with me,

    My life's been turned upside-down somehow.

All along I've been saying

     That I don't know what's wrong with me,

But I've known all along.

      I can't spend more than a minute

Without thinking of you

       And writing of you.

Don't get me wrong,

       I'm not obsessed,

I've just been flipped upside-down.

     Even though you make me laugh

Make me smile,

      Make my life so great,

I have to ask

    Just leave me alone

So my life can be the way it used to be.

     So I now know what's wrong with me,

I can't get you out of my mind,

    So please

IN RESPONSE TO AN ATTEMPT
THAT WAS WONDERFUL

My poetry is written
Because I cannot explain my feelings.
So I let my hand write whatever,
Then I read;
And then I understand.
Because you inspire me
You bring me unlimited joy,
And I'm sad because
Nobody has made me as happy
As you do.
You do not bring me any sadness,
Only a smile and well-needed laughter.
You are not selfish,
And there is nothing wrong with
Wanting a lot,
Especially when I can give it to you.
All anything takes is a little effort.
You only control three things in your life:
                    Yourself
                    Your actions
                    Your reactions
So if something does not work for you,
Do something about it.
Do you believe in love at first sight?
I am not sure.
I am happy you did
Because you did not want to
Did not have to
Did not need to
Are you being yourself,
Who you are deep down inside?
That is all I want

To be around you.
Do not be sorry,
You have done nothing wrong at all
I have never been sad all over,
I have just never felt this way before
And it feels different,
Which thoroughly confuses me.
Yes, you are only one person,
But that is enough for me
Because nobody will ever be you
Only you
For me.
If you would like,
We can write to each other forever
Your poetry invokes things great in me;
Things I have never felt before.
Have no worries,
Or they will have you,
And they will consume you or me or anybody.
No worries of boyfriend and girlfriend?
Tch . . .
I would rather the truth:
Let us just be friends . . . if you want.
That would be more painful,
But at least it would be the truth.
But I hope "just friends" never comes
From you,
Never from me.
I feel as I feel
And I wish you would, too,
Follow your heart
In these situations,
It is always right.
If you knew me better,
You would know that my innocence
Was taken from me

The day that I was born.
You have never corrupted me,
Only changed me for the better.
The opportunities I am kept from,
Which are not unknown at all,
I am not kept from at all.
So let the poetry flow freely,
Nothing halting at all.
And let us be selfish
Making the world work
Our way.
And let us not bring sadness,
But only peace and happiness.
And let us bring up anything
And let us never be sorry
Let us never keep our feelings
Hidden from each other's views.
Let us not be sad at all,
And only be ourselves.
Let us be surrounded
But keep ourselves from being crowded
And lost in this sea of unending people
Who hold endless possibilities.
Let us not be robbers of innocence,
Purity and pride
Or love or hate, let us not debate,
That things really could be worse.
Let us not corrupt and not keep each other in the dark.
Let us show each other light.
So let us write poetry to each other
Deep into the night
And let us have no worries of boyfriends and girlfriends,
Only cuddle on the stairs.
And let us be as we are
Who we are
Feel as we are

Act as we are
Never to please
Only to be
Never to die
Live on forever
Never to stop
Feeling our feelings.
And let us not bring sadness,
Only happiness,
Peace, purity,
And pride.
Don't despair
I will be here for you
When on a shoulder you need to cry.

LONG LIVE LIFE!

❈

So true so true
So true
Are words spoken
From the heart
All the whispers
All the utterances
All the little things
So little time
So many feelings
My hand won't stop
Oh so boring
When you're gone
Oh so quickly
When you're around
Deep mysterious connections,
No doubt
I feel it
I can't stop
Can't leave
Never want to go back
Always want to stay
Don't go
From my reach

APRIL 22

❋

No one understood
Me
And I thought no one ever would
But on a Sunday
A beautiful Sunday,
Those thoughts were turned to stone.
No one understood
Me
And I thought no one ever would
But I met someone who had a key
To more than just my poetry.

NOT SO SOON

❋

I am spent
I am tired
I am finished until tomorrow
Unless I feel it coming on again
Or if someone were to stoke my fire within,
Then, once again, I will begin.

HATE AND LOVE
❧

I think you hate me
I think you love me
I feel it deep inside.
Think about how much I've been inspired by you
Just in five short days.
Ask first
I do stupid things
You hate me
Want to break away from me
Never see me
Never be with me
I am with you
You love me
Want never to break away from me
Always see me
Always be with me.
I don't understand you.

FLIPSIDE

You think I hate you?
You think I love you?
You see it deep inside?
Think about how much you've been inspired by me,
Just in five short days?
Ask first
You haven't done stupid things?
As far as I know, at least.
I hate you?
Want to break away from you?
Never see you?
Never be with you?
     No.
You are with me?
I love you?
Want never to break away from you?
Always see you?
Always be with you?
Always.
I begin to understand?

INTERLUDE TO THE BREAKDOWN
❊

At one moment
I am one person
At another
I am another
Then I am interrupted hastily
While new nations are formed
I just want to cut off his beard
And take his glasses
Even though he tries to help me
Too hard.

Back to normal.

DO IT RIGHT
❊

Leave me alone
Oh leave me alone
Yes,
I hold a special place in my heart
That she liberated
For her.
Because of her
I gained my independence
But there were problems
It wasn't as easy
I was divided
I am owned by two
Wanted by many
Many

Left unsaid.
Raise your hand!
Be the only one who knows the answer!
Get it right
Feel the quiet
As you do
And feel the breaths
All released simultaneously
Get it right
Don't worry about getting it
Wrong.

UNTITLED POEM #31

There's so much dirt
Under my fingernails
From all my years on earth
It refuses to come out.

My past is so humiliating.
Only a few know even half of it
I keep it bottled up
Under my fingernails.
I wonder how many others
I think I know so well
Have as much to hide as I do.

UNTITLED POEM #34
✻

Everything great in my world
Ends so quickly.
Especially when they are the greatest
Experiences of them all.
Exhausting, they might be,
But those are the moments in time
That set me free.

UNTITLED POEM #36
✻

I can be anyone you want me to be
And more.
But I don't want to be.
I just want to be me.
Be myself.
Don't try to throw the ball.
Just throw the ball.

UNTITLED POEM #37

Someday
I will meet my match,
And someday my pen will die.
Someday
I will feel no more,
And someday my pen will die.
And on that day
I will be no more
Resting forevermore.
And I hope I will have said
All I felt to say and more.
Someday
I will live no more
And someday
My pen will die.

"If you don't try out new things, you won't find new things to do."

"I like staring out a car window at all the people sitting in their cars.
Even though they are all so sad, I see inside their eyes that
there is something greater."

CRY AND BEAR IT

The anticipation
is killing me
It hurts inside so bad
go away from me today instead of tomorrow
I want nothing more
than to uncork my hidden upset
And leave my hate inside.
things to take my mind away
To a place that knows no time
but none actually work in time
And as I sit here
wishing life were easier
And life weren't so hard
i forget about the times I've seen
What's in this world,
the real world,
The one that surrounds the bubble that we live in,
that keeps reality away.

HOW CAN YOU BE?

A windshield wiper's bold percussion
Penetrates on through my chest
Doing all the right things
Makes me feel so weird inside
Join the mind and the body
But nothing comes to mind
I only think that what I'm feeling
Is neither me feeling
All my feelings at once
Or feeling absolutely nothing at all
Or many feelings so confused
That nothing ever makes sense
Or one feeling that's so deep
That it would take days of blanks
To understand it.
Maybe it will go away tomorrow
Or after I take a hot shower
Or maybe it's here to tell me
That my dream of long ago
Has finally come true.
I feel so deprived of everything I want
And given everything I need
Talking so openly about things so private to me
I just want to close my ears
And shut it out
A hard fight every day
All the day
On every thing
Just takes so much out of me
That these feelings bring
A whole new meaning
To the words:
"I don't know"

MANY DIFFERENT FEELINGS
✳

Life sucks.
And that's all I can say to the people
Who ask why I am sad.
The advice I get doesn't help me in the least.
A feeling is in the air.
I feel it bulging in my stomach.
It makes me want her.
It makes me sting.
It makes me want to . . .
I feel so lonely
No one pities me
I hope for many things to come
I wish I wish I wish for oh so many things.
I feel a feeling,
That makes my heart start to rise.
I'd like to thank you
For all the things you've done.
I feel so, so, so tired . . .
Tired of all this time.
I sometimes can't get a word out.
I sometimes feel so scared.
I sometimes stick my neck way out
And feel like I can't care.
Sometimes I watch my step.
Sometimes I step without caution.
I always will be faithful.
I always will be driven to find.
I will feel for you as you will never feel for me.
I will never lose my energy.
I always feel grateful that you are here.
I feel hurt when he steps in.
I feel untouchable when he goes away.
I feel indifferent about my sticker.

I feel jovial when you are around.
I feel worthless when you're gone.
I feel justified when I'm told I'm right.
I am learning always.
I am merciful to people who deserve it.
I am merciless to people who deserve it, too.
I am merry when you are around.
I am nicer right after you were with me.
Who anyone is, is non-negotiable.
I am open to those whom I trust and love.
I sometimes feel overtaken by my feelings,
So maybe I should stop reading my works.
I feel rewarded when my patience and faith pay off.
I feel it as painful, you not being around.
I feel it's unjust and all, you not being around.

IRONIC

✷

Am I stupid?
Am I an idiot?
Do people run circles around me?
Am I not cool?
Am I not with it?
Am I not smart?
Am I not intelligent?
Do I not know what I'm doing?
Am I slow?
Am I uncoordinated?
Am I bad at sports?
Am I a bad speaker?
Am I a bad friend?

Am I a bad boyfriend?
Am I a bad person?
Do I doubt myself?

AND I HAD A DREAM

VERSE I

And I had a dream
That you passed my by today.
And you didn't say
A single word to me.
And I had a dream
That you would not talk to me
And you didn't say
That you were missing me that day.

CHORUS I

And I will always remember
That dream that I once had
But I know that it'll never
Turn sour because I know what's ours is true!

VERSE II

And I had a dream
That you refused to be with me
And you didn't say
That you really missed me, too
And I had a dream
That you stopped writing me
And I went on home
And felt like I could die that day

CHORUS I

And I will always remember
That dream that I once had
But I know that it'll never
Turn sour because I know what's ours is true!

VERSE III

And I had a dream
That I missed your warming smile
And I couldn't see
What was ailing you
And I had a dream
That I was never graced by your presence
And I went my path
Sadly, crying without you
And I had a dream
In which I couldn't see your face
But I could see
What love there was that was pounding in your chest

CHORUS II

And I always remember
That dream that I once had
And I know that it was true
And that I'll always be in love and true to you.

VERSE IV

And I had a dream
That I could see you were in love
And I had a dream
That you loved me always with all your heart

CHORUS II

And I always remember
That dream that I once had
And I know that it was true
And that I'll always be in love and true to you.

VERSE V

And I had a dream
That I fell in love with you
And I knew that we
Would live on growing old
And I had a dream
That I knew we'd be together
Now and ever
Late into those cold and lonely nights

CHORUS II

And I always remember
That dream that I once had
And I know that it was true
And that I'll always be in love and true to you.

VERSE VI

And I had a dream
That I knew that we would write
Our poetry
Now and ever
Late into the night

CHORUS II
2X

And I always remember
That dream that I once had
And I know that it was true
And that I'll always be in love and true to you.

NOWADAYS
⚜

Life is so hard
Pull down your shirt,
You're showing too much skin
With love
Pull up your pants
Become respectable
Go to school
Learn
Be good
Come back before 10
No sex
No girls
No boys
Drink more water
Don't drink
And don't drink and drive
Go to your room
Do your work
With love
You have so much
(Feels like so little)
(Deserve more)
I think
Deserve less
You can't wear that shirt
You look like a pimp
You look like a slut
Get off the computer
(Be there for me)
I'll be there for you
(Don't forget me)

love me
(leave me alone)
do your homework
with love

CHAPTER 7

WHEN IT BEGAN

7-ELEVEN
❊

split lilacs
down their middles
because they don't deserve
their own maidens of riddles.
Some might say
That things of such
Might be the way
You hoped and dreamed it may.
But don't think too much on those subjects,
Or they will become silent objects,
Sitting sadly in the back of your head
Many miles of thoughtful waters they will need to tread
Before they again will be led
To the frontal lobes of your heart-broken head.
But little lilies
And nasty narcissus
Will bite when least expected.
Make sure your indefinite perfectness is forever protected,
Or else the broken walls of empty kitchen wings
Will be detected, along with other things:
Little children stowaways,
Sitting scared and silently staring
At all the big mice and men passing;
Giant chalk-lines
Running merrily throughout the fields of heaven
As a burly truck driver asks for coffee,
Freshly brewed at seven-eleven;
A cockroach eats his own little feasts,
Running wildly from those nasty beasts.

DON'T KNOW, YOU?

❊

And the time is coming
The light is falling
Dark is coming
The love is leaving
And dark is setting in.

JANUARY 2

❊

Downward spirals
Have to end sometime
I sit in the back seat
Of this wild ride
Wondering where the lapbars are
Wondering when it ends
And trying to remember
When it started

COULD YOU BEAR IT?

What would it feel like
To be the man, "Ike"
Who dropped A-bombs
On kids and babies' dads and moms?
I would hate those
Dreams that plagued my energy redemption
As I would watch one face with attention
One face I watch of each I killed
With a simple atom with which a hunk of metal was filled.
Could you look in every face
Of all the people you murdered
For your country to save face?
So every night you go to bed
You will dream one face in red
At a time until you're in your final bed.

But there could be a state of mind
In which you might possibly find
A place in which your personal peace isn't timed.

TAKEN WHERE
✳

Boxers box
And dive as a fox
Don't give out
And only shout
When blocks of steel
Break out wine
To unend the stitches
On which platelets dine.
Pants will not be aware
Of all the tiny sticky hairs
Lovingly stroking their
Pantlegs held by belts up there.
Don't feel as though
Love is fleeting though
As fast as a rose, it'll go
Running in and out of all
The heinous things and will it fall?
Rent and take out things new and old
Only one at a time
Only simple and one-fold.
Those you take out will tell tales untold
As the stores you didn't buy from quickly fold.

Everyone else gets freedom
Everyone knows they need 'em
But how exactly do you go about
Finding that love that has no doubt?
Will it find it's way here?
Or will it wait for me to appear?
Or is it half-way across the land,
Crying hard, and feeling bland?

A VISION OF LOVE

✤

Little bat wings
Flying towards things
Only at night,
Scary in flight.
Frozen lakes on the go,
Nature protecting the rushing of "no".
Freeze big swans,
Beet red with love,
While all the spirals
Hover above.
Easy wishing friends
The rumor who pretends
To tick like a clock.
But after a knock
On this door with a lock,
It's shaken and stirred
To quickly be curved
And stumble into millions of spiders.
Half of whom run more wild
Than anything resembling a child,
And leave a trace tender
To be found by a mender
Of anything but hearts that are shattered
By someone who mattered,
But now has sheepishly battered
My heart, mind, soul,
Which are now sickeningly tattered.
But crosses cross
And O's go on forever,
As many little creatures
Cry, "Damn! Damn! Never!"

UNTITLED POEM #44

Ten little ducks
Sitting in a row,
Wishing there was somewhere
They could go.
Ten little baseball players
Sitting in a row,
Wishing there was somewhere
They could throw.
One little heart
Sitting by himself,
Wishing there was some way
He could get off his shelf.
One little boy
Sitting all alone,
Wishing there was anyone
Who wants to talk with him on the phone.

SENTINELS
⚜

Many sentinels, all in a row
No one knows where they'll go.
Doesn't little Teddy Bear
Know how to pay a fare,
Or does he only know how to care?
Can a dandelion roar like a bee?
Or can it only sleep like a tree?
Only time can say goodbye to these
Sentinels alone, saying only thank you and please.
Roads can travel far, far away
Until they reach the vanishing point
Never, tomorrow, or even today.

Someday birds will swim like cats
And someday fish will fly like rats.
Someday soon someone will say:
Sentinels please, break for a month and a day.

Someday shoes will walk unaided
Someday girls will have hair unbraided
Someday lives will live untainted
Someday science will cure people fainted
Of diseases still un-naméd.
Someday love will be perfected
Someday evil will be neglected.
Someday soon, all will be accepted
Someday soon, money will be depreciated.
Someday Sentinels will go untainted
Someday They will be perfected
And someday soon, won't be neglected.

SARCASTIC
❄

Smile sweetly,
It's all fake.
Please turn my clock back.
Now is not the time.
I can write two whole pages.
Three art.
I have nothing to impress you with.
Kiss me.
We should use this song
To express things . . .
But it's slow,
So change it.
It's old
And time to leave.
So goodbye
To the list of other times.
Everything is deeper than what you think it's depth is.
Do you have the time?
You make me
Laugh
Profess
Many truths
And loves,
But keep it *quiet*.
But please open me up to new things
Because it's healthy for me.
Whoa!
You can't be taller now,
The time is all wrong.
Because time is a long painful process.
One going in order
Upsets the balance
Of one changing the tempo of time.

So soon,
And yet so late.
There's always more.
But the chair is warm.
And it's too late.

REWIND
⚘

"Never"
Starts with "n"
And ends with "R"
I just wish
Never is not what we are.
But away far
Is my car
So far away is our
Love of all things!
Could you see it coming?
Or were you busy running?
I must stop my ever-flowing ink
Before I fall over pain's nasty brink.
Can you see a future in your mind?
Can a positive feeling in your heart find?
Can you love me 'cause I'm so kind?
Or on last night should Father Time rewind?

I TRY
⚜

I try
To figure out what you mean.
I try
To figure out who you are.
I try
To figure what you mean to me.
I try
To understand who we're meant to be.

Don't worry about the things
That are uncontrollable.
Don't fret about the people
That say we're not meant to be.
Don't listen to all the gossip;
I'm not who I am said to be.

I try
To understand what just went on.
And I try
So, so hard
To impress you and make you like me.

It's all for naught,
Because I know of you I'll not be free.
I travel down this road of uncertainty.
I wonder when I will be free.
Free from all the strife that for me you did find
And left to torment me and my,
Horribly wonderful, fretting mind.

I try
To figure out what you mean to me.
And what I might mean to you,
Which there's really
Only one answer true;
Namely me and heavenly you.

A LITTLE LOVE AND SOME LIGHT POPCORN

PROLOGUE

Kim and Jeff
Sitting in a tree
K-I-S-S-I-N-G.
First comes love,
Then comes marriage,
Then comes Tommy in a baby carriage.

VERSE I

When it began
I was unaware
Of all the things around me and about her.

CHORUS

Sometimes I wish that I was dead.
Sometimes I wish that we were wed.
They all keep laughing it up
I think that we're in love
Am I just infatuated?
I'm in love.

VERSE II

Many times a day
I think about the way
You swing your ass around town and I love it

VERSE III

I can't keep you out
Of my flying mind today
I wish that you would go away and quiet down now.

CHORUS

VERSE IV

They all keep laughing it up
It's time to give it up
I'm in love with you, I can't lie.

CHORUS

Reaching out to you . . .
But you never want me . . .

UNTITLED POEM #40

Fear is in my eyes
Staring at all that I despise.
I cannot look you in the eyes
For I don't know how I'll surprise
You and all your feelings
Stay true to you and you alone.
But I will always know
That you sit on my throne.
Never in my life
Will you from anywhere.
From anywhere be thrown.

And God acting witness
To my true confessions.
I promise you I'll stay on true.

But all my feelings tell me what I shouldn't say to you.
I know it.
I feel it.
I wish I couldn't ever say to you.
I feel you.
Believe you.
And all my mind will ever say of you
Is please her.
Relieve her.

BE REAL
⚜

A dead rose of pale complexion
Eating many a sweet confection
Cannot make the easy connection
Between bad health and a bad complexion.
But when a pencil wilts away
Yesterday,
And it's gone as soon as today
Rolls on by,
Waving hello and kissing goodbye.
Everyone knows that pens try
To be real fly.
But everyone knows
And it shows,
Pens die
And wave bye-bye!
Don't let the memories
Fade with the cemeteries
'Cause then we'll be
Nothing more than thin souls free.

DO YOU WISH
※

Do you wish
That I was more boyish?
Do you wish
That I was less foolish?
Do you wish
That you, I could nourish?
Do you hope for
Some hot guy to wash ashore
And over you love to pour?
Do you dream at night
For a handsome man
To turn into a shining-armored knight?
Do you wish of me
To love thee,
Or only for us to be
A lovely camaraderie?

Are we friend
Or are we foe
I love you,
Don't you know?
I wish you
Would love me so.
T.S. Elliot and Bradbury
Can't describe my heart's trajectory
Enough to cause it injury
Before it launches towards victory.
The victory being that heart of yours
That's been there since the dinosaurs.
I would be the champion of the world over
Just to break your corrugator
So you couldn't frown at me anymore.

GRADUATION ALL TO ITSELF
✻

And you're closer to
A little graduation
Getting the world
More and more inflation.
But it's all good
Cause I know you would
Sing your summer
Till it became funner.
Little sundrops
Jump and shout
Don't let those summer rays
Make you pout.
You're out for a lifetime
But it won't last a moment,
Never should you say:
'Never say never'.

But my congrats
Any which way.
I hope you have fun
Every single day.

A VOICE

*

On a stutter
Stands a thought
On which is formed
An idea
On which a voice is raised
In an opinion
On which is altered
A mind
While speaking up is
A voice
To change different opinions to become similar
In a meeting room filled with
Individuals congruent to none but themselves,
Coming to influence
The building of presence inside
A city abundant with
Life,
Creating and moving energy
To move,
        Change
The world
Surrounding
A city,
A building,
        A man
Alone
        With himself
Down to his similarity with none but himself,
In a room with
Different opinions becoming similar
While speaking up is
A voice
On which is altered

A mind
On which a voice is raised
In an opinion
Of an idea
Which is formed solely upon
      A man
Alone
          . . . with a bubble expanding out from him,
            separating him infinitely from everyone else
            because he is one.
With an idea
On which is formed
Stands a thought
On a stutter.

FIFTEEN MINUTES
⚜

Three years old, see two boys,
Staying happy with their toys

Well, here I go,
Off to school to-day . . .
Let us hope that things just may
Work out placidly just to-day.
"Teacher, teacher, what makes things nice?
Eating milk or fish with rice?"
      "Tell me, dear, what may you say
When your mommy puts food away?
Will your mommy run away
When mommy puts the toys away?

When the mailman dines upon your door
Will you ask your mommy for that much more?
And when you grow tall and oh-so-wide,
Where will mom be when you want to hide?"
      "Teacher, teacher, can't you see?
Sometimes your words just recognize me.
I cannot break my happy days;
A young'n can't hold back in only five ways:
        'One for catnip hanging high,
        Teasing letters milk's alphabet sigh.
        Two for flying air-e-oh-planes,
        They sigh by like bowling lanes.
        Three for rats that run dead in cages,
        Just like blank words on black pages.
        Four for the fiddler on the roof,
        Once you grow, his image goes poof.
        And five for the silent boys who always hide;
        And five for the old McCoy pushed to the side.'"
Here comes time for budding thoughts
With rain that smells like desert droughts.
But no way can my bread become lunch . . .
Let me tell you, it's just a hunch.
There may not be a speed bump in Montana town,
But "whatever" when I tape my eyebrows to go up and down.
      "Teacher, teacher, can't you see?
I've lost my own identity.
What can you do to solve the bee,
Spell it, smash it, set it free?"
      "Tell me, dear, what's a lie
when you find it, knot a tie,
make a rainbow with a spoon,
fly that lie right through the moon?
Can you tell what make you are
When you look up close, so far
Without a thought to falling leaves
Or thoughts of your jacket's burning sleeves? . . . "

I know my loins are not yet grown,
And my heart is not yet sown,
But I feel a lengthy tour
Is meeting here to ask 'what for'
And challenge worth with butter knife
As smooth as mirth, as long as life.

      ". . . Some may say you'll go to waste,
Others say that boys eat paste,
Walk with vigor, walk not haste,
Walk with smiles on your face;
Eat with dignity and pride,
Show your daunting smile wide;
Throw the ball a thousand feet,
Make a smile for the beat
Of the hum that is your song
Take a while, have a seat,
Make that smile not too sweet . . .
. . . But here's the door to lock the key
Just don't say you heard it from me:
      'One for catnip hanging high,
      Teasing letters milk's alphabet sigh.
      Two for flying air-e-oh-planes,
      They sigh by like bowling lanes.
      Three for rats that run dead in cages,
      Just like blank words on black pages.
      Four for the fiddler on the roof,
      Once you grow, his image goes poof.
      And five for the silent boys who always hide;
      And five for the old McCoy pushed to the side.'"

               ✵

Seven years old, see two guys,
Swatting away the tiny flies
               ✵

Here are the staples standing strong,
Banded together, they're lasting long . . .
Name the Pharaoh of my mind
With a dog's tail in a wind,
Cannot think and cannot dine,
In Italy comes the greatest wine.
Time to come and a dime to go,
Time for rum and a lime to throw
At the mailman dining here,
He's eighteen and drinking beer
The beer of my mind agitate,
The rumbling inside is just so great.
What's this feeling; what's this noise?
Teacher, teacher, what is poise?
She might say with hair all white:
"It means not to start a fight!"
But I don't believe in ghosts,
Only in responsive hosts
Who live inside me causing; trouble,
And's gone before it settles, rubble.
    "Teacher, teacher, what's that sound?
It's beating me round by round,
Living does not change
A backwards cap that's out of range.
When the backdrop fades to black
Where'll they go, what will I lack?"
    "Listen, dear, there is a key,
But it's one you do not see:
      'Life has meaning, life is mind,
      Light is beaming, light can find
      Anything that you may wish
      From eating milk to rice and fish,
      But it takes time to bake the air
      To make it taste like rainbow hair.

This hair will blow the breeze of head
And heart, self, soul into one wed,
And there you have it: state of mind . . .
Go have fun . . . what will you find?'"
One of me may not bake well,
But break the bread and it will sell
Said someone great and someone loud,
Someone sound and someone proud.
Make the date and don't regret
The things life brings, please do not fret
Asks all the people who have lives
And all the men who have nice wives.
    "'Teacher, teacher, can't you see,
Life has thought like you and me.
It can breathe and it can see
Water, colors, grass so green,
But why can mommy be so blind
To the clouds that must rewind:
        'Life has meaning, life is mind,
        Light is beaming, light can find
        Anything that you may wish
        From eating milk to rice and fish,
        But it takes time to bake the air
        To make it taste like rainbow hair.
        This hair will blow the breeze of head
        And heart, self, soul into one wed,
        And there you have it: state of mind . . .
        Go have fun . . . what will you find?'"
Now I have to eat a pig,
Playing games with one old twig
On a lamppost of my love,
But I'm seven; mom is love
To the friends I do not have
When time has met its match.

Thirteen years old, see two men
Questions crowing like the eye of a hen

Can't we all just get along,
Frolic part of happy song?
Here, there, chug-chug-chug
Go the trains that brainwaves lug
Many an atom with family on the brain . . .
Different split middle, going insane.
        "Teacher, teacher, can't you see?
Life ain't as nice as it seems to be
When emptiness brings rings around
The world I've recently sane found,
Walking dogs and wearing a cap
While my inner child lies down for a nap,
But what's this feeling, deep inside,
Now I know it's bona fide."
        "Son, listen up, so you can see,
Time is playing games with me,
Now is not the time to grow,
Think of carrots in a row:
                'One may feel a need to break
                Away from those who may seem fake,
                But pacifist's rage is not for you,
                Above the sun, telling true.
                The laughing love we think is all
                May be real, you make the call.
                On which spoon in the sky
                You decide to try
                In the porridge of a lie
                Made to make us try
                Our best on every dragonfly.'"
I can feel the wind blown secrets near,

Pulling at my in-turned ear,
What I hear is squeals insane,
Pleading deaf to have a name.
I blindly sense the song of fall,
Winding down this aimless hall,
But why do I have to be mad?
Why do I have to be sad?
From where do these feelings journey,
Will they bring me on a gurney
To a place so far away
Where I can frolic and I can say:
There may not be a day that I
Stop to think of that dragonfly,
Under wing, but we're out of rye,
Who dares disturb my inner-song?
Am I awake? It's been so long.
And here we have two jolly blokes,
Lost, unnamed, without their folks,
Or anyone of any importance to me,
Because now these opposites are finally free.
Why haven't I thought of this yet?
I think I know, I think I'll bet:
I bet that life was simple, simple till one day . . .
Simple till one pimple came rolling down the way.
A pimple of my mind,
Two, in fact, you'll find:
One for all the goodness: peace, purity, and pride,
He's all for great big smiles, caverns open wide!
For two, the hate's a stainless steel tank
That damned the sucker to rob a rake with a bank!
To show this mindless malleable teen
That a new love is in the air:
No more is 'different' to be seen
As weird below the hair.
     "But teacher, teacher, can't you see?
Sometimes your words just recognize me,

Now I feel a power deep,
Waiting to break out of one long sleep.
But before this war is fought,
Let me try one last-ditch thought:
       'One may feel a need to break
       Away from those who may seem fake,
       But pacifist's rage is not for you,
       Above the sun, telling true.
       The laughing love we think is all
       May be real, you make the call.
       On which spoon in the sky
       You decide to try
       In the porridge of a lie
       Made to make us try
       Our best on every dragonfly.'"

ᴣᴐ

Fifteen years old, see two men,
Inside crazy, outside Zen

ᴣᴐ

Oh, hell break the butterfly
Back to maggots that always cry
Because life never need
Any more a place to lead.
My elevator cannot drop
Any further now to stop
In time for the anthem brutally
Butchering my desire thankfully.
Cannot we all just die one night
And leave this pain without a fight
To end the dinner of the postman,
Who was eating cardboard roast lamb
On a stick of death, destruction

Using nothing but the suction
Of the charred lips of a martyr
Who won't be there to see you later.
   "Teacher, teacher, can't you see?
The pressure bulging so inside me?
Won't you care to hear my story?
I must say it's quite the gory!
   "One side says to break the ways
   Of the old, outdated days.
   To end the blasé life so bland
   And start anew on richer land.
   A land of broken times of hate
   Leave room for the mailman to debate
   The absence of freedom, the absence of love,
   And no laws stopping the death of a dove.
   Side two says to stay the same,
   Become an angel without the fame,
   To be ridiculed for choices brave
   And to free the breath that was a slave
   To broken times of lies
   That all but hate despised
   And that is all beginning
   With the former who is winning.'"
Time the blasted souls who hurry
Through a passage marred with fury
Leading to another time
Of etchéd expletives of little thyme,
But no one cares about the time!
There is no right, nor reason, rhyme!
And I slash my withered arm on through!
The faces of our daily lives,
The mermaids' chests are all in hives
For the breaking news of storm
Inside myself so sticky and warm.
   I lash out with sudden hate!
Lies! The words of sullen fate!

I am searching for a twisted glory!
Push me to delay my death!
Close my pawned, fake, final story!
Rape me from my final breath!
Why was my life ever-downhill?
I feel like wood inside a sawmill:
Cut up like a man un-made;
Nothing but a deuce of spades!
In a game worth nothing more!
Than a nickel and dime store whore!
How does one suffer just enough
To create the mind to fill and stuff
A bag of hate held tight by fury,
Tainted by the poison fury
Of an angel whose wings are broken,
And his voice felt so outspoken?
He had nowhere to go one day,
Except inside himself, per say,
And all that's left of that little boy
Is a memory in a stomach's toy,
Gurgling many holy prayers,
For some revealing taxi fares
To bring back the child whom love had held,
But now he's filed, jailed, and celled
For the burning desire to hate
Anyone with time to debate
That stomach with feeling, feelings of hate,
And teacher, teacher, where are you?
When I need your words so true?
I hate the words you told at me!
And the laugh you hurled at me!
But where are you to help me now?
All I have is feeling wow!
In my feathered hell of pain!
Making my world spin insane . . .
Die on the day you were born!

I am full of insatiable scorn!
For all you ever taught at me!
And God!! Give me the power free!
To break your heart in pieces three!
Hear my proclamation lie!
On the ground with a single dying hell!
And I expel! . . . with unintentional peace,
Something leaves, something ceased,
While my time-wary brow is creased,
I think of nothing but a pleasant feast
Full of postmen frolicking
And the mermaids walloping
In the simple morning light
Of a sun just out of sight
But I can tell it's just around the bend,
Because I know friendships do mend.
In time together are two men,
Who watch another life begin
And laugh at the course of things again
As the world turns 'round again.

THURSDAY, FRIDAY, MONDAY

A brick, a brick
In the walls that we create;
Where do they come from?
Where do they become fake?
      Hurl them to the ground
With the power of knowledge,
But what good do the foes do
When they're sick inside the head?
With mother does one
      Time the race with
A watch without a face,
Who will get it right?
Wholly provocative are the blasé words
Of pacifists on a rampage
Because one would not think
A pacifist to flip.
The depraved jaybirds poke amicably
At the unsavory entertainment
Yet to be entertaining.
But when I lift my eyes to someone
I trust with timeless thoughts
Deep inside my self-contained artificial heart,
And when I lift my eyes zealously,
I make the skies wonder why
They did not make my eyes green
And my hair blue.
Capriciously I think of her
Whenever I am ill and never when I'm not
Because of times remembered and hard times all forgot
On the days that time is never standing
Still to consternation suddenly with
Apparitions slowly coming to a
Light.

Time has no constraint on the dead.
Lime in a drink turns faces red
On the same plain that books have read
About their obituaries of letters unsaid.
And parents yawn while their children led.
Light: an abusive, corrupt profit without concern
For unwise oddly placed tasteless impulsive changes of mind.
Never find the lucky few who's fate is to rewind
The stone legs of Prefontain with Mercedes yet to find
The tape recorder of our lives with a little recollection of the mind.
Light the path
And hence forth History repeats undulating topics to me
And you swoon onto your desk with dreams of being free
To not have life or love and no responsibility
To save the lives with punches to the face that you can't even see
Because depth isn't one thing that the teachers let me see.
Light the path to sleep
Dying are the bright, luminescent cloths covering my broken soul
With a thought to an inane and nonchalantly ostracizing mole
Upon my face with laughing consternation for my unsheathed and bloody
soul
Without a single thought to what may come to be its goal
To follow with the pride and strength of a woman's standing soul.
Light the path to the sleep of those who
Have a mouth ferocious with the down-turned, saddened corners high
Contemplating sorrowful reality with the fascist mouth a sigh
In to the journey of a million thoughts into a tongue defy
The many baseboards assuming things about this crossed-arm lie.
What sense does hair make when it turns those pursed lips so they're dry?
Light the path to the sleep of those who are
Broken music records lying heaps of garbage onto my dinner plate sad
With the bleeding pen of yesterday's thoughts of friendships mad
And timing the bells of heaven to the horns of devils and a truck's fad.
Why do those who never tell end up being close to those who are glad?
And why do sneezes come at random with the thought of God and a lad?
Light the path to the sleep of those who are tired.

Sight the bath to the beep of those who are hired.
Fight the laugh to the leap of those who are fired.
And time the soul with a stopwatch.

ODE TO MISS MCKAY

⚜

Miss McKay
Give an A
To the student whom writes true
To all the little raindrops and you.
Stay through
The boring lectures to
Eat alone and welcome you
Into the thoughts
Of days of "nots"
While technique and water bottles
Are controlled by many throttles
That heat up hot
When forgot,
Reading a textbook
Which has new stuff that at I can look.
I remember days
In which I was in a daze
And life was but a haze.
But writing got me there,
Weather nice
And weather fair.
I'll not forget you,
My writing cataclysm,
The sacred teacher of Journalism.

WHO'S RIGHT?

Can one ever really tell?
Unless someone lied about the length of their beauty
Or a broken ruler on a plain.
What do whispers really say?
What does the fact that nibbles always reach
The ears of unwanted Tom's at the wrong
Time tell us about the doings of the wind?
Where bathing in great beauty glistens
With the sleeping mother's decadence,
One asks all of them:
      Where does the red fern grow?
      On Tom's head or in a row?
      Do lilies stay sober from happy nights
      Or leave later with cuts from fights?
      Does a butterfly shed when the lights are off
      Or does she lean on the porch when you are gone?
      Why do the children ask those things
      About Tom's lilies and dragon's wings?
      Who may tell the children of pressure's power
      And the bad time's black, high, scary tower?
      Where does the free bird roam on through
      And why do your ears ring just by floor two?
      Bring me a thought or two,
      Leave them by the door.
      I will walk with you,
      Asking time for more.
Who *does* retain the right to chain children's purity
And innocence to the floor?
Who *does* hold the power to call up Tom?
      And ask him what has made one wrong?

MY MIND STUCK ON THE VERGE

⚜

War is on the verge
Of my mind.
Advancing rapidly
Towards the centers of my thought.
Not even the soulful sweet song
Of a pretty blue parakeet dancing dutifully down, down, down
Can clear my mind of a mouthful unsaid
Being left lonely and sitting silently,
Raging rampant throughout my tattered battlefield of a soul.
The sun sings that the new night is begun
After only so little time from when
The man in the moon ate the cheese
And committed suicide,
Declaring a decadent day of deformation
Was damned from day one.
And only after an amazingly atypical day of analytical assignments
Was the beautiful beginning of a new nanosecond
Never not ending only for a simple short second.
Love being boastful and dying down, down, down
The lovely little lane of Sam's boutique
While on a whim I sit, wondering when the blue parakeet
Will wish without withholding well-wanted, well-needed withering
information.
Does anyone ever easily intimidate intricate imitations that imperfect
Many men meandering methodically? Maybe I mean many musicals
Dilly-dallying down, down, down,
Demanding deeds from damned, demented souls
While the white witch withdraws willingly without wanton wishes
As I can't contrive of competently conceiving correctly
The horrible hell that lives deep, deep, deep inside
Laughing lengthily at losers like me.
Looking longingly lengthwise at the long twisted features
Of someone sadly receiving the nasty news

Of a feeling forgotten.
But only not omitted for reasons kept concealed
Is the pretty little parakeet spinning silently down, down, down,
Meeting meticulously in the midst of many mongrels milling around us
Only for a simple sweet second surrounded quickly by stupidity.
And the idiocy intimidates inane intentions
That only can be timidly talked to with towering twisting tongues.
Only for a precarious precious point on a timeline
Do we meet magically,
Touching together not before ever or never forever.
Only for a second in time.
A simple shoe, too tantalizing to not try on, lies lazily.
But the knowledge of never knowing what would happen,
Could happen,
Simply should happen,
Is too tempting to flee freely
Without witnessing the war eating everything up.
Will the pretty little parakeet win?
Will the pretty little parakeet withdraw?
Will the pretty little parakeet willingly admit defeat?
What might happen to our pretty little parakeet?
He needs petting.
What should I do?
What should I do?
Left or right
Or right or wrong
Never right nor left nor wrong.
The pen always sits teetering dangerously on the
Quickly rising, ferociously flying, fence of
That little joke of jokes being left by that magical man in the moon.
A two-sided ball comes hurtling hurriedly,
Ready to aim towards me at any moment the parakeet with the backwards hat
asks.
Be very careful which side you jump to.
It's your clean call.
But call clearly because wait . . .

The answer always arrives at the appropriate time.
Don't jump too soon or too late.
Everything always at the same simple time.
Impossible.
Everything cannot always depend upon chance.
But it does!
Some get it.
Some don't.
Some do.
Some don't.
Those that do, do.
Those that don't, don't.
You?
Ask the pretty little parakeet anything, if you trust him.
That little loser will willingly withdraw opinion
And tell the falling man in the moon
Exactly what he wants to hear.
The pretty little parakeet wins, doesn't he?
War is on the verge
Of my mind.
Advancing rapidly
Towards the centers of my thought.
Can the pretty little parakeet ever conceive of contriving consciously the careful
Countermeasures calculated to correctly chance the change to
Complete the can of corn that can keep calling Caroline to
Contemplate the cautious, creepy, caring, condescending,
Conditions that can complete the killer cycle of cheesy comedies
Careening cautiously towards the carefully contrived collage
Of care, curiosity, and clear, complete, concise, correct, and collective
Feelings?
The parakeet asks for heavy help from on high,
But gets no reply.
Didn't someone say simply not to spy?
And of course, our parakeet defied
And did not abide
To the rules of this racy realm of rural rides,

Going here to there and back.
The man in the moon yearns to yell to the
Cheese and the parakeet
Before he willingly wins the war within,
Either committing suicide by easy accident or
Hopping home happily hand-in-hand with her, the
Blue parakeet psychotic with the backwards blue hat,
Which is unusually new-looking.
It symbolizes a clean clock.
The little parakeet recollects readily the recaptured
Image of the hat's defeated features when he told her that
His clear, complete, concise, correct, and collective feelings
Were for a blonde Carolyn parakeet
When they weren't.
And the dead director disremembers to decide whether to direct or die,
Which leaves the sun crying gray shrouds of sorrow and
The moon mourning over the misleading megamall of
Major misgivings.
Don't forget to smile, pretty little parakeet.
Hide those unimportant realizations
With finicky false feelings of a fake reality
That you wish would appear with a hug and a kiss.
One way or the other.
Never both.
Pretty little parakeet and some cheese,
You can't venture back over the forgiving fence
Because, in a real reality, that fence never forgives,
And you know it.
You only refuse to believe.
Try not to stare and drool so much.
That touch was not for you, my friend.
It was only there as from a friend to nothing but a fine finite friend.
Don't forget what she yelled at you for.
That was for you.
How that blue parakeet with the backwards blue hat opened your sleepy eyes
With her magic potion of tantalizing truth.

But it's always longer on the right path.
Always harder.
And the cheese won't ever not taste of a greater importance than it really is.
But you can always forgive the other fighters for what they did wrong.
Pretty little parakeet,
Things look different when you finally finish the hateful uncertainty
And realize that you're in love.
Things look different when you open your eyes.

AS I LOOK BACK
❊

What happened to me?
I'm so different . . .
In a good way.
Great way!
I'm so . . . so . . .
Different!
I cannot put it any other way!
Thank the Lord,
Wow

LAST DAY

All the hate, love
Well inside me
To think of all the
Times you loved me
All the cool trees
All with a breeze
Shading me from a hot freeze
Every day I please.
I can't remember
Any time since September
When we weren't together.
But now that damned day
Has arrived again to say
"Now it's time for friendship to lay,
And wait for three months and a day
Until the time inevitably will arrive
When scholastic matrimony will once again
Give us the five
And give us the drive
To start again with friends forgotten
And begin anew with friendships rotten.

HELLO AND GOODBYE

Welcome to my show
and everything is alright.
It's finally time to go,
but everything will be alright.
Turn to page once again
to keep me in your sight,
Or put me away for good,
either way you will be right.
But now I bid you farewell,
with a thank you and a nod,
I'd love to stay and chat,
But here now stands the night.

A MESSAGE

This is a message to those of you in doubt:
"If you have something to say, just shout
but do not use a violent way
or a mean way at all,
just turn the volume up a bit
and brace for flight and fall."